The Self - Helpless

Pandemic and the Life Eternal

D1823263

P C Mathur

XpressPublishing
An imprint of Notion Press

XpressPublishing
An imprint of Notion Press

No.8, 3rd Cross St,
CIT Colony, Mylapore,
Chennai, Tamil Nadu - 600004

First Published by Notion Press 2021
Copyright © P C Mathur 2021
All Rights Reserved.

ISBN 978-1-63886-171-3

Preface

The pandemic may have left some people feeling helpless, like there's nothing we can do but wait for the worst.

But that's not true. In fact, there are plenty of actions you can take to help those around you, and yourself – and to feel like you're really making a difference.

Sometimes in anxiety-producing situations, it can make a big difference to feel like you're taking action to help.

Even in the face of isolation orders there's a lot you can do – including some acceptable reasons to leave home.

This is an unusual time for all of us, but it's a time when we can channel our worry and uncertainty into real actions that can help our friends, our neighbors, our community and ourselves.

The life is eternal. Life can only be extinct on earth due to interplay of cosmic forces which incident may be millions of years away.

A mere 2 gram of virus (This is the total reported approximate weight of Corona virus afflicting the entire world) cannot decimate the life on earth.

We do not know our-Self.

We do not know what is going on about six inches above the base of our necks.

But we know what went wrong when Chandrayaan 2 travelled approximately 4 lac. Kilometers with Vikram lander but missed landing on moon by four hundred meters.

We know what went wrong when Voyager 19 which landed at Titania, a satellite of Uranus, three seconds off schedule and hundred meters off course after a flight of six years.

We are the strangest creatures in the universe.

Mental pressures are ruining our lives. Share your concerns. Give help and seek help.

And that is self-help.

The epic Bhagwan Gita admittedly is world's first self-help book. Arjun suffered from the mental illnesses which today would have been given fancy names by modern medical science.

Arjun's plight was exemplary. Only he knew what hell he is going through. There were mightier warriors than him in his army who could have easily annihilated the Kaurawas. But no one came forward to take up the cudgels on his behalf and relieve him of his misery.

His psychotherapist Lord Krishna had to step in. Gods are supposed to destroy evil. But why he himself chose not to do it, is not understandable. Why Arjun, why not the lord Himself. He could have obliterated Kaurwas with a flick of his finger.

May be the lord developed cold feet.

Arjun needed time and treatment to get over his depression. It took seven hundred Shlokas and as to time it is said to be frozen during the period Gita was taught to Arjun. It implies zero time.Gita is a third person account - by Sanjaya to Dhritrashtra. Though it seems irrational but "absolute truth is beyond space and time." The great Einstein said this. Krishna is a character, historical or created and conceived as absolute truth.

Epic Mahabharata is full of pointers to issues of psychiatric dimensions and offers many answers. Lord Krishna can be considered as the first celebrity counsellor. His sessions with his patient Arjuna led to his spectacular recovery. Thus the history of psychiatry began five thousand years ago. There were no psychiatric drugs or mental health professionals at that time. Five thousand years ago nature was at its most beautiful - pure water streams, serene rivers and oceans, birds chirping without fear, trees swaying in the wind, deer prancing around in your backyard. This had its own way of healing an injured mind.

Mental blocks (OCD etc.) and real trauma can be treated only by a professional. No self-help literature (including this book) can really cure you. The grim fact is that only a sufferer of mental problems, depression, anxiety, unknown fears, panic attacks and a host of other horrible conditions knows what hell he or she goes through. Sage advices and other measures of this kind don't help most of the time. Consult a doctor and a specialist who will prescribe medicines which will bring back the chemicals that are flowing inside your brain from the wrong to the right pathway.

The self-help industry is a multi-billion dollar industry. It fills bookstores and conference rooms. It's made media celebrities out of people and capitalized wildly off the growing self-consciousness of recent generations. And although it's changed the lives of millions of people for the better or worse, I assume — it still lacks a certain credibility with most. Many laugh at the bizarre superstitions that get passed off as legitimate life advice. Many try self-help out but are left feeling helpless.

Clinical psychology doesn't exactly have a stellar track record of personal change either but it is better than others. But at least when you sit before a mind mover you know you're dealing with a qualified expert who is telling you what to do based on 100+ years of empirical research.

Self –help is a market-driven, rather than a peer-reviewed industry. The onus is on the reader to sift through the material and decide what's credible and what's not. And that's not always easy to do.

The following are five major problems with the self-help industry today, and they're unlikely to go away like corona.

1. It brings feeling of shame and guilt

Two types of people get addicted to self-help material: those who feel something is fundamentally wrong with them and they are willing to try anything to make it better, and those people who think they're already generally a good person, but they have some problems and blind spots and want to become great people.

These people are of two categories.One who think themselves as "flawed to normal people and others as "normal to great people" First group of people are in it because they believe that they're fundamentally flawed and want to fix themselves. Normal to great people are in it because they think they are OK, but they want to become great.

Generally speaking, the OK-to-Great people do just that — they go from having an average and "OK" life and over the course of years turn it into great or so they think.

The Bad-to-OK people improve little, if at all, even after years of "effort" In some cases, they may even get worse.

OK, why?

Bad to normal people consistently fail because they possess a fundamental worldview that interprets everything they do, including self-help, to support their inferiority or lack of worthiness.

For example, an OK-to-Great person may read a book and think,

"OK good, there are a bunch of things here that I'm not doing. I should try them out."

A flawed to normal person will read the same book and say, "Wow, look at all of this stuff I'm not doing. I'm an even bigger idiot than I initially thought."

The fundamental difference is that Bad-to-OK (inferior to normal) person lack s self-acceptance that most people have. An OK-to-Great (normal to great person) will look at the string of bad choices and mistakes throughout their lives and decide that they should make better choices and learn how to be a better person. A Bad-to-OK person will assume every choice they make is bad because they are a fundamentally flawed person and that the only way they can make good choices is by doing exactly what someone else says, word-for-word.

The irony here is that the pre-requisite for self-help to be effective is the one crucial thing that self-help cannot actually help: accept yourself as a good person who makes mistakes.

Sure, sit with your Chi, be still in the "now," say your affirmations and journals until you're blue in the face, but Bad-to-OK people will continue to perceive themselves as "Bad" and never reach the "OK" they're desperately looking for. Because this inadequacy is their worldview, everything they do will only reinforce it further. At best, all they can hope for is to cover it up or suppress it.

2. Self-help is often another form of avoidance

People consciously perceive their problems in all sorts of unique and creative ways: I don't know when to scold her; my family and I always fight; I feel tired and lazy all the time _I can't stop eating sweets; I can't stop smoking,I have strong urge to go out in lock down and on and on.

These all feel like "real" problems. But in almost every situation, the root of the problem is actually some deep form of anxiety/neuroticism or an unconscious feeling of shame or unworthiness.

We already saw how self-help usually proves ineffectual in dealing with the shame. Unfortunately, it often fails in handling the anxiety/neuroticism as well.

When someone with an inordinate amount of anxiety comes across self-help material, two things usually happen, and neither of them fix the problem.

(a) They simply replace one neuroticism with another, slightly healthier neuroticism — think someone who goes from being an alcoholic and unable to hold a job, to meditating and doing yoga five hours a day and still unable to hold a job.

(b) Or they use the self-help material as another form of avoidance. Doing social work or joining an NGO are classic examples. Let me prepare myself for these things. A great high of achievement sets in. I start reading books on these things. But since your heart is actually not in this but suggested by a self-help book, not knowing what my basic nature is, I read one two three and four books on these themes, entangle ourselves in it and finally end up in shame and depression.This is known as analysis paralysis.

3. Self-help marketing creates unrealistic expectations

Although theoretically, I have no issue with the profit motive in the self-help industry, but in practice it causes problems.

With the profit motive, the incentive is not on creating real change but *creating the perception of real change.*

This can be done with placebos, teaching people to suppress certain negative feelings or to pump their temporary emotional states. It can be done by placating anxious people with more information and neurotics with more relaxation techniques. These all create short-term sensations of accomplishment and improvement, but almost always dissipate within a few days or weeks.

I'm sorry, but you're not going to get over a lifetime of feeling inadequate or shame in a single weekend. You just aren't. What *will* happen is you'll feel better about that inadequacy and shame for a weekend and then it will come back again with greater source.

4. Self-help is usually not scientifically validated.

There are the self-help practices which have been shown in scientific studies to have some validity: meditation or mindfulness, keeping a journal, stating what you're grateful for each day, being charitable and giving to others.

Here's where the science is hit and miss (it usually depends on how or why it is used): Neuro-Linguistic Programming, affirmations, hypnotherapy, getting in touch with your inner child etc.

Here's what complete nonsense is: Fengshui, manifestations, tarot cards, telekinesis, psychics, crystals, power animals, tapping, and the law of attraction, anything supernatural.

The fact is that the majority of self-help information out there is either a placebo at best or complete bunk at worst.

Fortunately, in the past decade, many academics such as Berne Brown and Dan Gilbert are getting into the mix by writing self-help books based on scientific studies, rather than the usual trope of "I was cleaning out my closet when God spoke to me and I suddenly became enlightened and here's my completely arbitrary and half-baked book on what you should and should not do with your life."

5. Self-help book is a contradiction.

The contradiction of self-help is that the first and most fundamental step to growth is to admit that you are OK as you are and that you don't necessarily need anyone else's help. It's the prime belief and by its very definition, it's something that can't be given to you by someone else, it must be reached on your own.

The irony is that once you *do* accept that you don't need someone else's help or advice to become a good person, it's only then that their advice truly becomes useful to you.

So in a way, self-help is most useful for people who don't actually need self-help. It's for the OK-to-Great people, not the Bad-to-OK people, although those are most of the people who get caught in its net and spend their money on it.

Self-help is quite literal in its meaning — it's used to enhance oneself, not to replace it. If you're looking to replace who you are with something else, then you will never succeed, and you're more likely to get sucked up into the nonsense and pseudo-science and suppress your feelings of inadequacy rather than deal with them head-on.

In other cases, self-help allows people to transfer and project their feelings of inadequacy onto others, or live vicariously through a "Guru" or someone else's success. Again, it's the perception of progress and not progress itself.

So what's the point of all of this?

Further self-help learning can be useless. And here are five reasons why.

1. Lessons Learned Aren't Applied

It's easy to read a self-help book or attend a 'life coaching' seminar and gain satisfaction just from the dopamine high that comes with finishing a book or reveling in the highs of the seminar.

But consumption is the easy bit.

Putting the lessons into practice, making changes, and executing requires an order of magnitude more effort, and that's when the wheels fall off for most people. Oftentimes, it's not the lessons that are inherently useless, but people's non-application of them that makes them so.

2. Asymmetry in Circumstances

As Nobel Prize-winning physicist, Richard P Feynman puts it:

"If we run an experiment in a certain place in space, and then run the same experiment at another place, then whatever went on in one place, in a certain order in time, will occur in the exact same way in another place in another point in time, provided the features of the environment have not changed."

When it comes to taking advice from self-help books, symmetry only exists if the circumstances surrounding the author's success, or the case studies they present, were the same as yours when the described action obtained a given result.

One must be objective when reading books and evaluating how this might apply to one's own circumstances, and how it might not. A startup founder could read a book about how IBM reinvented itself, and while they might take some lessons from it, it's unlikely to teach them much about, say, raising capital for a new venture. Similarly, some business advice may have worked in the 1990s, but the world has changed much since then thanks to the internet, and many lessons may no longer apply.

3. Narrative Fallacy and Survivorship Bias

We tend to attribute our success to what we would rather remember than what we would rather forget, drawing a straight line from start to end, rather than the squiggly line that is truly representative of success.

When we read self-help books from people who have scaled the summit, it's easy for the book to be full of very specific things that worked, while discounting the things that weren't as obvious — the failures — but were just as instrumental in getting to the top.

Not only that but for every successful person who followed hypothetical steps one two or three, there are probably hundreds who did the exact same thing but failed. This is partly to do with power laws and the nature of the universe, and partly to do with luck.

Finally, correlation does not equal causation. So while an entrepreneur might credit action X with result Y, it could have just have been a result of the myriad other actions that were in play at that point in time. Scientists often confuse the two — by accident or deliberately — so you can sure as hell bet that your Silicon Valley tech brother does too.

4. Luck

Like the narrative fallacy, it's easy to attribute our successes to how awesome we are.

The fundamental attribution error, a human bias, sees to it that when we make mistakes, it's because of our circumstances and when others do, it's because of their character.

But what we often neglect to acknowledge is the role that luck — good and bad — plays in the success and failure of both ourselves and of others.

Sure, we may have done lots of right things on our way to the top, but per survivorship bias, you can do all the right things and still fail. Oftentimes, you also need a little luck to be on your side.

5. Bad Advice

And yes... bad advice. Many self-help books amount to hastily written business cards that are full of anecdotal advice and 'because this worked for me, it'll work for you too'. Such anecdotes can be subject to confirmation bias, cherry-picking, luck, the narrative fallacy, non-replicability, asymmetry of circumstance, or just plain old nonsense.

The reality is that everybody's circumstances, capabilities and goals are different. There is nuance in our lives and in our respective pursuits.

And a simple one-size-fits-all piece of advice usually fits nobody.

Rather than expecting one piece of advice to change your life, observe widely and you will begin to see patterns emerge. Advice that tends to stand the test of time and run the gamut of literature. Apply it and see if it works for you. If it doesn't, move on to something else. If it does, do more of it.

Most of the other stuff included in the various material is really just filler. Stories about the persons' life, how they overcame adversity or stories of other such people and their challenges. Which is great, it's all really inspiring and motivational stuff but when you've heard one story you can usually guess what is going to happen with all the rest. The protagonist has a tough beginning, goes through some hard times then changes their life around to become a huge success. Why Do We Consume Such Content? Now I know what you must be thinking, "If you're so annoyed about people doing well for themselves and turning their lives around then why did you read and listen to so much of their content!?" First off, I'm not hating on self-help books and similar content. I believe that it's extremely useful and can really help change a person's life for the better. The issue for me — and I guess for a lot of other people — is that it can become quite addictive in a way. It may sound ridiculous but it is true. I'd finish reading one book and then race down to the book store to get another. Upon finishing an audiobook I'd be on the online store buying and downloading another. At times I would buy three or four at a time, books and audiobooks, just to add them to my collection. As mentioned above, this is something I have been thinking about lately and one of the questions that I asked myself was, "Why did I spend so much time reading and consuming all that stuff?" Especially since all the core principles are basically the same, as I said previously. The conclusion that I arrived at was that I — like so many others — was searching for a shortcut to success. A magic formula. The blueprints to a new life. But in looking for something so specific I had failed to realize that the answers were staring me right in the face each and every time. The path to success was; Work hard Stay focused Never give up Do whatever it takes Don't Waste Time. Take Action Now!

Self-help books and content can be very useful on your path to a better life but don't fall into the trap that I did. Sure, read and consume the content. Take inspiration from the stories. Use them as motivation but also take action while doing so. I got so caught up in the consumption of all this great material that I forgot to do the most important part. Put the knowledge to use. Nowadays I still listen to and read the work of such influencers but mainly for entertainment purposes. They say you are what you consume so I like to have the message of these positive people in my head as much as possible. Using them as fuel when I am working out or when I'm in need push on the back on days where I'm less motivated and feel like slacking off. Self-help books — like many other things — can slow you down. But only if you let it. Use them as the tools they were created for. As motivation for you to achieve your hopes and dreams.

"Knowing is not enough! You must take action.

It's this: find out for yourself. That may sound silly but seriously, why would *anyone else* have the answers to *your life* but you?

You can take their experiences and ideas into consideration, but ultimately it's their application to *your life* that matters.

None of this was supposed to be easy. Anyone who tells you otherwise is probably marketing something.

Be skeptical. Be selfish. And be ruthless. This is your life we're talking about. Nobody else can be happy for you. If you find yourself having that expectation, well, then there's your problem. And no one can help you except yourself.

I feel very bad as I remember all those years I wasted practicing self-help... practicing all the different techniques, implementing the lessons taught by the so-called experts, and, not to mention, spending all my time reading about it. That was during my most productive years of life. Unfortunately It was all a waste. Not only did I not really improve myself, I made myself even more miserable, even more lost, even more alone. And I know now most successful people don't bother using any complicated formulas as suggested in these self-help books. They never try hard in life. They just hang out with their friends and family who keep them in check and who help guide them to get what they want from life. That makes all the difference in the world.

Being introvert I rarely made friends. The few activities I enjoyed were of a loner nature. So without a Common interest I did not get friends to walk with me understanding my unique temperament. So I had to tread my path alone. This was the beginning of my depression phase. I developed inferiority complex And shy of mingling with people and the few friends I did make while growing up were isolated themselves or tried to isolate me from others. I can only guess that they had their own insecurities that made them act this way. But, eventually, we also broke ties. That left me all alone. That left me to figure out life by myself, which is always a bad strategy at best.

In my self-help journey, it was me alone in my room reading a book or a magazine or torn bits of old newspapers. Of course, these things promised the world or I thought it contained some good information worth having. It was exciting and compelling stuff to learn at the time. It was both pleasurable and entertaining. How could I ever stop? But that's part of the game the self-help book industry plays as they want you to get you withdrawn into your own imaginary self-help world to become even more isolated. (I should warn you, just about all of the self-help industry is very toxic with a lot of miserable people. You would be wise to stay away.) And when you're isolated, it's easy to convince you that bad ideas are good ones and that you're an incomplete person without their advice. And the few times I did take action, even when I followed their advice to the letter.

But my results were bad to mediocre at best. This would just cause me to retreat even more into self-help trying to find the answer to my life. But as the years went by, no real progress, no real change. Isolation really is the dream killer.

If you're reading this book, I imagine it probably isn't the first self-help book you've picked up (but if it is, lucky you).

There's a lot that is said in self-help. I don't know how anyone can expect to effectively remember or use it all. Sure, you'll find common themes in all the books (which will make you feel like you're on the right track), but even that is too much to remember. Even if you could, how can you make sure you'll use or remember that information when you need it. The answer: you won't. And even if you do remember a few things so you can apply them to your life, how do you know if there aren't better self-help strategies out there, if the strategies you could come up with on your own aren't better, or what if it is these strategies that are actually holding you back in life?

It's no coincidence that there are a lot of successful people out there who have never read a self-help book. Or, if they did, it was something where they said "that's nice" after reading it and moved on to live their lives without giving it a second thought. And it's no coincidence that the few people who consume self-help like a starving man at an all-you-can-eat buffet usually end up going nowhere. That's not to say self-help isn't useful, but, rather, taking action and being with the right people is all that really matters in life.

If you're reading this book or other self-help material, you probably need a plan that will do just that. You need a simple strategy. you can always remember and easily apply so that you not only start changing your actions but also start to actually live your life, a reminder to do what all the normal, successful people already do without thinking about it. And I'm going to give it to you right now. Here's the secret, if you can call it that, you've been searching for in self-help. It's called the three steps. You don't even need to read the rest of this book for it to work. This is all you have to do in life:

THE THREE STEPS:

> A. HELP YOURSELF
> B. ASK FOR HELP WITHOUT HESITATION
> C. OFFER HELP TO OTHERS

That's it. It really is that simple. Stop thinking life or how you have to handle it is harder than it really is. You don't need a complicated system to have a good life or to get what you really want. Go ahead and write it down. While they sound like common sense, to align your new actions with these steps you'll need a reminder (as, apparently, you haven't been doing these steps or else you wouldn't have turned to self-help in the first place). Keep it in your wallet, in your purse, or on your wall so you don't forget. Really, I'm serious. Stop reading and do it right now. If you can't do that simple task, you'll never break your self-help addiction. This is all the self-help advice you need.

But with respect to how you do these steps is for you to figure out on your own (the rest of the book is basically dedicated to me proving this and offering a few ideas here and there). This also means you don't need to read any other self-help books. No, there aren't steps you need to follow to get what you want from life (they probably give you that many steps so you'll get trapped in their world of self-help where you keep giving them money for advice). That's just way too much information to actually use anyway. Self-help people do like the word seven: "Seven Habits of...", "Seven Secrets to...", "Seven Strategies that...", etc. Funny how it's always seven. It's almost like they're more interested in making a marketable book instead of helping the reader... But even seven is too much to remember to effectively put into practice. But with the above mentioned three, there is no way you're going to forget it: help yourself, ask for help, and give help to others.

So how is this different from all the other self-help material proliferating there? It's different because it really isn't self-help. Two of the three steps are focused on other people. You're getting help from others and you're helping others.

That really isn't self-help at all. I included the first one as no one is going to break into your room, drag you out, and force you to interact with the world; you have to help yourself first. And that's really the best thing you can do for your life: focus on others. Isn't that ironic? The best self-help advice out there is to not do self-help. Don't do self-help; instead, focus on other people. Let them help you and you help them.

Sure, you should do things for yourself to be healthy and active (eating the right foods, exercising, being social, etc.) and do the things that you find interesting, which you'll improve at with time as you do them more and more. But stuff like that should come naturally (at least if you're the type to be reading this book).

You don't have to fundamentally change yourself. You don't have to "improve" yourself. You're fine the way you are. You just need to change your focus and point of view. You need to put your focus on other people, not yourself. But only when you accept yourself can you really start to the put the focus on others. And if you're really pushing to improve yourself, then there is probably some unnecessary insecurity you haven't dealt with.

Yes, some insecurities will always be there to a degree (that's just being human), but they often only serve to hold you back. However, a good way to forget about and get over those insecurities is, oddly enough, to start focusing on others. Again, don't focus on self-help; focus on others. But focusing on others is a bit of an art, a skill you develop over time. But at the same time, it's not as if you haven't been interacting with others your whole life. It's really about learning to let your natural abilities loose in your current situation. And that's where the three steps can help. They'll keep you on track and act as a reminder to practice this skill so you'll get better at it. So how do you go about helping yourself, asking for help, and helping others?

You help yourself by getting out of your room, going after your big dream in life, applying for that job or quitting your current job, making that call, having that talk, putting in the work, practicing that skill, going to that group activity, making a good friend, sending an invite, leaving a toxic situation, not doing things by yourself, ending or starting that habit, being brutally honest with yourself, letting yourself have some fun, etc. Asking for help is exactly as it sounds. It might be hard and scary at first (as is helping yourself), but the more you do it the easier it will get (same, again, with helping yourself).

So keep asking for help with the things you are trying to help yourself with. Finally, give help to others. People need help, everyone needs help, but you often have to ask them what they need help with first. People might not have the courage to tell you, so you need to find the courage to ask. And you should give to others as it makes you a complete human being. It's what you're really looking for in life. But, remember, you also need help as well. Don't let yourself be. alone with your problems. Don't trap yourself with self-help. Don't let yourself be isolated when it comes to your dreams. You need people. You might say, "What about all the details, exceptions, and things to look out for when you implement these steps? Won't I need this valuable information?" You don't need to worry about the nitty-gritty. You'll figure it out as you go along. The important thing is that you start doing the three steps.

The important thing is that you start taking action. Even if you read about the details ahead of time, you won't internalize them where it'll be useful. Yes, I'll go over some ideas to help you better understand the main concept, but I'm not going to hold your hand and go into every possible situation you might come across. That'll be a waste of my time and yours as knowing about and using the fine points in life can really only come from experience. It's like an athlete only who knows how to play their sport better by playing it over and over again.

Advice from a coach can help guide them, but only experience will make him or her a better athlete. Besides, I think trying to understand the details is where people get hung up when it comes to self-help, instead of getting the experiences they need firsthand. The details are definitely interesting to read, but are they useful? Not really as you will all too soon forget them. And, too often, people stress about remembering and using them instead of taking action. Experience is really the only way to internalize and get better at something. You need to just focus on doing what needs to be done. You need to focus on taking action. Speaking of which The Three Steps Help Yourself "Take action" a phrase is found in just about every single self-help book sold on the footpath. That should tell you how important it really is. But what if taking action is the only self-help advice you really need in life. That would make the rest of the self-help industry rather pointless and penniless.

I think taking action is so important that I put it at the beginning of the book instead of at the end like most self-help books. Better to try stuff out, like the three steps, and learn as you go, which is really the only way you do learn in life, than to read and never really use any of the information. I'd rather have you close this book right now and take consistent action instead of reading it and going off to another self-help book.

How could taking action be the only advice you need? Well, it really comes down to the fact that we're all individuals. Sure, you could take and apply what you learn from a self-help book in a systematic way. But that advice worked for the author, it doesn't mean it'll work for you. It could even harm you. Even if it seems to do you some good in the short-term, it might ultimately ruin your life in the long-term. The best way to learn if you should do something or not is to do it and then think about the experience on your own (not blindly trust self-help material). The best way to improve at something is to do it over and over again. The best way to improve any situation is to do something about it. The best way to learn about yourself is to do something new. The best way to find out if something will work for you is to do it and see the results. Don't waste your time over analyzing or researching trying to find the perfect way. You won't find it.

But a better way will always show itself to you from taking action. You could argue any trick or system is bad for you. You could even argue the three steps in this book are bad for you and that you should just do your own thing.

In defense of the three steps, it seems like it is simpler and the more focused on action and yields better results. I don't think it can get any easier than the three steps. And they're uniquely used by everyone as people have to come up with their own ways of applying the steps. They're actually more of a reminder to be proactive in life rather than a system to follow. But if you can think of a better reminder or way of thinking, go for it.

However, I would at least start with the three steps. And, hopefully, one day you'll let go of self-help altogether. When you start forging your own path in life, you'll start figuring out what is good for you. And you forge your own path, you figure out what is good for you and what is bad for you, by taking action, not by reading self-help books. Yet, that doesn't mean you just do whatever. You don't try everything in life once (you'll probably die if you do). But you also don't just keep doing what you've been doing because it's easy or in your comfort zone. You have to try new things in life. But with that advice, here are a few ideas to keep in mind when taking action.

Use your head. You have a brain. Start using it. You don't need a self-help book to explain everything to you, to think for you. You don't need me to hold your hand. You have to learn to stand on your own without self-help. If you know something is bad for you, then don't do it. If you know something might be good for you, then test it out. If the results come back how you didn't expect them, then take time to think about it. In the end, all that matters is your own thoughts about life as those are the only thoughts you'll use. Don't use someone else's thoughts on life as your own as they probably won't work in your situation (unless they are in a similar situation, so advice from a friend or peer might be good stuff for you to try... ask for help).

For the most part, you need to figure out things on your own. So ask yourself why your experience was bad or different than expected and ask how you can make the results better or if you should even bother doing it again. It's not about blind action (doing whatever you're told in a self-help book), it's about smart action. Use your head and think for yourself. That's how you start helping yourself. Trust your gut. But you don't want to think so much that it prevents you from taking action.

Thinking is usually best left after you've taken action, but you also don't want to take action that might harm you. So what do you do? And with there being so many options in this world, it's easy to do nothing at all or to think you have to try it all out. But like I said, that last option will hurt you and it might even kill you. So, again, what do you do? You trust your gut. Admit it, every time something bad happened there was probably some type of gut feeling you ignored. You're a lot smarter than you know. You just have to tap into that inner intelligence of yours. Yes, take action. Take lots of action. But you have to trust your gut before you take action as it'll not only help keep you from taking the wrong action, but it'll also help you take the best course of action. Trust your feelings. Trust your gut. Plus, your gut will tell you in a split second if something is a good idea or not and you can then act on it immediately.

But if you use the logical part of your brain, you'll burn a lot of time and energy planning and researching things that might ultimately end up being useless. Use that part of your brain after you've gained experience to analyze things, after you've taken action. Don't live completely in your comfort zone. There is nothing wrong with being in a comfort zone; you need it to keep sane in life. But being in discomfort is necessary to grow and learn about yourself. You have to try new things. Staying in your room with your computer and TV all the time, or whatever you have, isn't going to do you any good in the long-term. In fact, it'll do you harm in the long-term.

You have to start giving up your current comforts you can just give up some of them or just give them up for a little bit, you don't have to do it all at once and start putting yourself to really improve your life in the fast lane. That won't work. You don't have to at once throw your computer and TV out of the window. You just have to take action on a consistent and selective basis. You have to try yourself by putting yourself in an uncomfortable situation once in a while where you might grow and learn new things. Sometimes it pays to meet adversities head on. You need to put yourself in an unfamiliar or unusual, but safe, situation where you will most likely gain from it. And that's what helping yourself is all about. That is often what they mean when they say "take action" in a self-help book. It's scary.

It's always a little scary no matter who you are or how many times you've done it. But if you keep doing it, it gets easier to face that fear. But spending all your time in your room will just make things harder again. Your fear will grow. You just have to keep doing what scares you, as long as you also know it's good for you. Whether that be registering for a new class or a business, meeting a violent boss or coworker, an angry spouse, attending that party you were invited to, applying for that job, going to the gym, going out with some new people, or meeting your new neighbors, or some unknown fear. You just need to do it. Sure, you might not enjoy it, but you will still learn something about yourself and about the world around you. You'll learn more about what you don't like, what you do like, what is good for you, what is bad for you, and what will get you results. But you only discover that from experience and experimenting, not from staying in your room.

You have to be willing to give up your current comforts to do what you know is beneficial or what you think might be beneficial for you. Expand your comfort zone. If you're not willing to make a sacrifice here or there to try new things and do what needs to be done, your life will never improve. Take your time. That means take your time. I'm not telling you to do it crab like and I'm not saying to do it when you feel like it or as hundred meter sprint. What I'm saying is that it will take time to get results. Understand and accept that fact. When you learn a new skill,(forget if you have jumped sixty -my apologies to senior citizens if parliament mandated that you are an SC after sixty years when you were born.) it doesn't come to you right away. You're really bad at it at first and sometimes you don't feel like you're improving at all, even though you are. So don't let yourself get discouraged, especially in the beginning. Just tell yourself to take your time repeating the process because in a few days or even a few weeks you're going to see improvements. Helping yourself by yourself takes practice, just like any other skill. But you will improve if you keep at it. So don't let yourself forget to do it and don't let yourself get frustrated so that you end up quitting. Relax. Just take your time and keep at it.

The truth is anything you work towards you will get, at least to some extent. Qaynaat- (nature) will help you. Whether that be a new skill, social status, a new career, money, name and fame etc., You will get it eventually. That means you don't really need self-help to get better at something or to improve your life; you just need to do the work. But you only have so much time to give, so don't waste it reading self-help. Self-help is a big industry nowadays like drugs. You know drugs are bad but people still take it. Thus, the question becomes, not whether or not you'll get it, but rather what should you be dedicating your time to? As you read this book, I think you'll see the three steps as definitely being worth it.

Be honest with yourself. Honestly, it can be hard to be honest with yourself. Why? Because you can get all caught up in these different worlds that distract you. But there is really only one world there, the real world. And when you escape from reality to avoid your problems they grow. You binge watch your favorite TV show. You play that game for hours on end. You read those self-help books. The reason the self-help world is so addictive has to do with the fact that they do speak truths about this world, at the very least warped versions of them. But knowing these truths won't mean they'll help you. Most likely you'll do nothing with them and they'll just get you stuck in your own little world, you'll get stuck in your head. And if you're being honest with yourself, you'll have to admit spending too much time within your head, driving your neural pathways out of their naturally assigned lanes making you sane looking insane. There is a very fine dividing line between madness and genius. So instead of taking action, you get yourself in a mess.

I landed in the same mess. Trust my personal word, trust my experience.

So in the first place don't waste your time with self-help paraphernalia. Again, there is nothing wrong with being in your comfort zone and doing enjoyable things up to a certain point. But there are a lot of things to distract yourself with and no one is going to tell you to stop. No one is going to come to save you from yourself. So you have to save you from yourself. You have to help yourself. It's your life; no one is going to change it for you.

Not your parents and relatives, not your friends, even foes and, definitely, not your government. You have to save yourself. And a good way to break away from your fantasy worlds, to see the big picture that is your life, is to slow down and reflect. Take a break from your distractions and take time to ponder what you should be doing with your life. That's the best way to figure out the action you should be taking, what you need to do to help yourself. You need to take time to reflect on what's important, on what you really want from life, on what makes you excited to be alive, on what makes you feel alive, and on what needs to be done.

If you don't know your motivation in life, not what your parents wanted for you, not what you think society wants from you. You do need to serve society, but the best way to do it, is to have tons of energy to serve, to find your inner motivation. You can't change your life as change has to come from within, not from some self-help book. Remember, you're a unique individual so your desire will be different from everyone else. And motivation can't be implanted, it can only be discovered. That's why you need to find your motivation, and with it your willpower, to change your life. Find your true motivation in life, your true dream. Find that and all that's left to do is to take action, not read self-help material.

You often read self-help because you don't know what your true motivation in life is. But reading will just leave you more confused and confounded. That is what I think. To find it you must look within. When you know it, you'll just start working on it, not read self-help. When you know it, you'll know that you know it. It'll be a burning desire within you. It'll be like a raging fire you can't put out. And you need a burning desire/dream to change your life. And if you don't have one, you're pretty much wasting your life. You need to get in touch with your true motivation in life. So find your motivation in life. Help yourself.

But you might need some time to explore this idea. And I see you arguing that I should have included reflection as one of the steps. But doing the three steps will naturally get you to start reflecting on things as you have to decide on what you need to do to help yourself with, on what to do in the real world. The three steps will often have you take a break from your distractions. And a break will also naturally have you to start to reflect on life as that's all there is to do. I really bring up reflection as a reminder to stop spending all your time playing games and watching TV (as they'll keep you from reflecting and they'll keep you from doing the three steps). Plus, putting some direct focus on reflecting is often needed to make sure you aren't fooling yourself. However, you shouldn't have to reflect too much on what you really want from life, as you've always known that. You've just let yourself forget. So it shouldn't take too much time to remember. But there is something else you should reflect on.

Before I tell you that, let me give this analogy. Life is a lot like a super over in cricket. You have only six balls to play at the end of your tether. You cannot make more than six mistakes. So what you should also be reflecting on is your past failures and how you could have prevented them, how you can fix your bad bat swing. Sure, your successes might have a common theme in them, but more often it is just luck that the situation called for one of your strengths, prior knowledge, and/or preparations (and you prepare by practicing/taking action, not by reading self-help). Failure, however, often happens because of your immaturity but all immaturities can be fixed. I know you might blame or want to blame something external for your hurt or failure, like a person, a unique circumstance, or something besides yourself. But bad things happen to everyone and bad things will continue to happen to you. Whether they become failures or not is all determined by your reaction, or lack of it.

So if you can become more mature in your response, you can prevent and even turn those situations around. But it won't happen overnight. However like a bat swing, you can slowly improve your maturity if you work on it. And I can guarantee you that your failure, your immature response, had something to do with letting yourself stay in a bad situation (not helping yourself), not communicating about your situation (not asking for help), or putting the focus way too much on yourself (not giving to others). But, like I said, how you do the three steps is up to you to figure out. And you either learn from the past or you repeat it. So reflecting on the past can be a good thing, but don't let yourself get caught up in that world. Don't relive your past. Learn from it and move on.

I think a good way to keep from getting stuck in your head about it is to get it out of your head and onto a piece of paper.

Do a simple writing exercise where you list your major past failures and then list the things you could have done to prevent them from happening or to fix them. Pull out the main themes you see so you'll know what to work on, you'll know what to practice on for a better life. Now you're thinking for yourself instead of just believing what a self-help book says. Then destroy that sheet of paper so you don't keep thinking about the past. If anything, this exercise will probably show you how important the three steps really are. Now that we've looked at your past, let's do another writing exercise with the present. Write down what is most important to your life (your friends, your family, honest relationships, hard work, freedom, adventure, building a better community, building a better life, etc.). Then write down what you did today (or yesterday if it's early in the morning) to live out what is most important to you. Or did you even bother that day to live out what's most important to you? Do your current actions align with what you really believe inside? I think most of you will see that they don't. But the good news is that you can start right now by taking action, by helping yourself.

You can keep repeating this exercise if you think it'll help keep you focused on what's most important in your life. But in the theme of keeping things simple, I would just write what is most important to you at the top of the sheet of paper with the three steps. Finally, let's do a writing exercise about your ideal future. Write it down. No matter how crazy it is, write down your idea of life as long as it doesn't include something fictional like magic or superpowers. After that, write down what you did in the past year to work towards that better life. You may not get it, but you will at least get some of it if you work towards it. If the answer is nothing at all or very little, then you know your actions aren't what they should be. You can keep this piece of paper that shows your ideal future. Or you can write the gist of it/combine it with what is most important to you at the top of the sheet of paper with your three steps. I am not going to have you write down your plan on how to get your ideal future as I'll show later in the book that that's a bad idea. In short, you should only plan with other people in achieving your dreams. But I'll talk more about that later. And I think that's enough with the writing exercises (but please do them). They're basic enough to let you know if you're on the right track or not in life.

But we don't want to get too crazy here as writing can also become a form of escapism. Taking time to reflect is often the first action you need to do. Just don't get too caught up in reflection or you'll just get lost in your thoughts the same way you can get lost in those other worlds. Losing in your thoughts may show you as a morose, long faced, sick looking person which will not be liked even by your dear sons and daughters and other close kin. You are likely to be kicked out of the house sooner than you think.

And getting lost in your thoughts is what makes self-help so deadly in the first place as you end up not taking action. Don't do that to yourself. Talking to someone about, or during, your reflection is a good way to keep from getting stuck in your head. Never underestimate the power of good communication. Be honest with yourself, you need to be putting more emphasis on action, the right action at least, instead of pondering things. So take a moment to reflect, take a moment to be honest with yourself, to figure out the right action to take and then take it. Once you get an idea, try it right away, test it out immediately. Feedback from the real world will let you know if you're on the right track or not. Then you can reflect some more on that new information and try out some new actions.

Will you experience pain when you start interacting with the real world chasing after your motivation in life? Of course, but, and most important of all, you'll also learn from it. So don't waste time in your fantasy worlds. Focus on doing. Focus on being honest with yourself and take action. Be in the moment. And speaking about self-help being destructive to you getting results and not living in the past, let's talk about being in the moment. We focus way too much time on the past or the future. The only thing that exists, the only thing we can take advantage of, is the present moment. I know it sounds spiritual (and, yes, the spiritual self-help industry loves to talk about this), but even if you look at it with simple logic, it's true.

And if your religion makes you wary about using any concepts from the spirituality movement, many religions covered this idea way before they ever did. The spiritual talks about not dwelling on the past and not worrying about the future. And it covers how God is with you in this very moment. But it also talks about the need to wake up and take action in life and not be lazy with your limited time on earth. Help yourself. But for those who aren't religious and don't care to read about the subject, don't worry I won't talk about it again.

And I think this shines the light on one of the main problems with reading self-help. We often read it because we are focusing on "fixing" our past failures or we're planning for our ultimate future, even when we know it'll probably just stay a fantasy. We often let ourselves escape reality by planning for a delusional life imagining what it'll be like or by rewriting our past in our fictional worlds. Either way, we aren't focused on the present so we can't take advantage of it or really get anything done. Why should we focus on the present? First of all, like I said, it's the only thing that really exists. Next, you can only really take advantage of your current situation by being aware of it. If you're focused on some future plan or past hurt, you'll miss the current opportunities right in front of your face. Finally, there is a genuine happiness that you get when you engage with the real world. Sure, those other distracting worlds are addicting and, thus, hard to give up, but they can't compare to the real thing. And you can tap into the real thing, the real world, at any time by being in the moment.

Don't underestimate the power of the present moment. While I can certainly understand thinking about past events over and over again, unfortunately, it won't do you any good. If anything, it'll leave you in a bad mood and distract you from taking advantage of the present. The best thing you can do is to learn from it and move on. To illustrate the point, I want you to think of your life before you discovered self-help. Despite your childhood being good or bad, I'm certain you had some of the best times of your life back then. Sure, it probably had to do with the fact that life was newer to you since you were younger.

But a bigger part of it had to do with you being in the moment. You weren't thinking about things as a child you just did things you liked. You didn't have all those weird self-help ideas going through your head. You didn't search for answers (read self-help) or give yourself big questions to think about which isn't always a bad thing but everything has a time and place. You just enjoyed the moment and found the answers to life when life was ready to show you. Bottom line: self-help keeps you from being in the moment. Again, you could use that line of thinking to not do the three steps. But they are really just a reminder to be a good human being, to communicate, and to be proactive in life, which will benefit you if you do and harm you if you don't. You were, after all, miserable enough to turn to self-help. So if you stop doing self-help and go back to your old ways, you'll get more of the same results. That's why I recommend you keep a reminder close to you at all times. Put others first, communicate when you need help, and don't let yourself stay in toxic situations.

So how do we be in the present moment? This might surprise you, being in the moment has to do with accepting yourself, it's because you don't accept yourself is why you run off to fantasy worlds and try to improve yourself. If you accept yourself, the good and the bad, your strengths and your weaknesses, your successes and failures, your good luck and misfortunes, your genius and your mistakes, and forgive yourself and let go of your ego, there is no reason to not be in the moment. In a way, you accept life and yourself unconditionally. And when you accept life unconditionally, all that there is left to do is to be in the moment. But that doesn't mean you do nothing. Instead, you do what is best for you in the moment. That's how you know you're in the moment. Whether that means just enjoying the people around you, relaxing on your sofa asking for help, working on what you like to work on, working on what you need to work on, or taking that chance in life, that's how you let yourself be in the moment.

You cherish what you have before you, your current opportunities and enjoyments, right here and now. You don't spend it lost in your head or searching for answers that deep down you already know. Doing is how you get yourself to be in the moment. Thoughts and distractions will just keep you from it. Actually, I think the three steps are more of a reminder to be social with the right people and in the right way as good friends will help you be in the moment and accomplish great things more so than anything else in life. But it's up to you to get out there and find them. Help yourself. In a way, you take complete responsibility for your life regardless of what life has done to you. When you're able to take complete responsibility for your life but you're still able to forgive yourself for your past mistakes your life starts to change as you free up time and energy to start changing it. When you take complete responsibility for your life, then all that there's left to do is to act.

And if you're doing something that is stressful or that seems overwhelming the best thing you can do is to be in the moment. If you try to use some gimmick, some memorized material, or try to think about and apply everything you know on the subject in that moment, not only will you probably fail, but people will wonder what is wrong with you. It is best to act in those moments with a beginner's mind

Act as if you're discovering the art for the first time, doing it with an open mind...hopefully, you can see how self-help material gets in the way of that. Do that and you'll subconsciously draw on all the knowledge you have while enjoying the moment and while making new connections and executing them on the go. You'll perform at your best. And best of all, you'll be true to yourself. Being in the moment is often described as getting out of your own way. Another similar, down-to-earth, non-spiritual way to look at it is to stop thinking about life and start living it instead. Stop living in a fantasy world and start living in the real world. And getting out of your own way means not wasting your time reading self-help.

"Talking about stress I will try to give you some scant but true medical idea as to what stress does to your body in the long run. I am not a medico but the facts have been culled from the works of international experts in psychology and psychiatry"

The study of the role of stress in causing diseases and their handling was first initiated by Carson and Selye, both world renowned physicians. They found straight and clear relation between stress and disease. They observed that there existed direct relation between various organs of the body and mental stress. Dr Selye in medical terms defined this phenomena as "the nonspecific response of the body to any demand made upon it ". They collected enough evidence to show that the organic functions of the body changed upon change in the mental state. Dr Selye found conclusive proof that the change in emotional state of a person brings about a change in the function of various body organs.

Many ailments have been identified as having their source in a person's thought process. In fact thought patterns are responsible for malady in almost every body part of a person. However not long ago central nervous system was considered to be a rigid and unmodifiable director of the various paradoxical reactions of the bodily systems. Now it has been learnt that the central nervous system is also susceptible to psychosomatic damage.

Largely mental stress is responsible for the following diseases.

1. Digestive

Anorexia Nervosa, Peptic Ulcers, Ulcerative Colitis, Irritable Colon, Cardio Spasm, Spastic Colitis, Nervous Vomiting and Diarrhea etc.

2. Cardiovascular

Angina Pectoris, Coronary Insufficiency, Essential Hypertension, Tachycardia, Arrhythmia, Vascular Headache etc.

3. Respiratory

Asthmatic Wheezing, Bronchial Asthma

4. Endocrine

Hyperthyroidism, Diabetic Metallic.

5. Skin

Urticaria, Warts, Neurodermatitis , Prunus Psoriasis

Ref: The Lancet

You can search social media for the details of the above diseases. However this browsing social media for health information terrorized me. It appeared that I have all the diseases there are and all the medicines have deadly side effects so much so that they kill more than they cure and everyone in the world is a qualified medico. I will advise you not to search the web for medical information. It may give you the shivers and make your life miserable. This knowledge or no knowledge is the nemesis of mental peace and biggest disservice by the social media specially the proliferating blog writers. Don't read them.

Sometimes ignorance is bliss.

Consider the example of the autoimmune disease Rheumatoid Arthritis. It has been practically proved beyond doubt that psychological stress plays a great part in aggravation of this highly debilitating disease.

Medical science underwent a revolution in the early eighties of 20"Th. century. Before that role of psyche as a factor in physical diseases was universally downplayed. However due to seminal work of Walter Canon and Hans Selye on the psychic causation of stress and its role in bodily functions with the advent and success of holistic medicine as one alternative approach with the recognition of mindfulness in preventing and curing of organic diseases as well as with the series of advances in neurophysiology and clinical psychology which go, a long way towards explaining the above insights. The recognition of the importance of the mental and spiritual factors in fighting illness has grown into an imperative of medical treatment all over the world. Maybe all these practices help to bring back your blood pressure to normalcy.

Prince Charles during those days in his official capacity as the president of the British medical association called for a thorough review of treatment and research in the area of connection of brain and brain working and physical diseases. Connection of mind and matter was found to be inseparable. He called it as a 'personal factor 'of the patient.

This was the royal idea of self-help (sans self-help book).I don't think he realized it but he started quite a revolution in the world of medicine.

In the US the miraculous cure of Norman cousins and others from serious diseases such as cancer through attitudinal healing brought the question in the realm of science.

But every revolution moves slowly in the field of medical science.

It is subtle to prove that the pain has just been caused your spouse's spat with your neighbor.

However a way exists. This is to gain first hand experimental understanding of the deepest level of your mind and the ways of mobilizing your spiritual resources whatever they mean. Ask someone and test the levels (of spirituality) as you cannot test your own level.

Certainly a self-help book cannot do this for you.

Raising positivity of thoughts has been found to cure or prevent diseases.

When one is emotionally disturbed, the organic disturbance is not seen immediately. If organic illness followed every emotional disturbance there would be no need of this book. Rather the organic illness by itself would have taught us the great lessons of the need to retain emotional balance and would be masterstroke of self-help.

The reason is this. Our body has been given extra capacity by our maker. We have been made with a safety factor of 1 to 5 and more in case of certain organs.

Our heart possesses five to six times capacity than normally required.

Thus when our heart function falls below five to six times its strength, likelihood of heart attack will arise.

Likewise if we remove about twelve feet of our small intestine out of 22 feet we will still have good digestion.

In the same way we can do with one kidney all our lives.

Our bone marrow can increase the production of red blood cells almost seven fold if required.

It follows that every emotional disturbance does cause change in our body systems and reduces the attacked organ's reserve capacity.

And when all of our organics are depleted, we do suffer with the manifest disease (clinical case).This process of depletion may take many years before clinically visible.

Psychological stress acts as slow poison. Take notice that one must not be wary only when a disease is manifested. One should make all effort to preserve the body's reserves by leading an emotionally stable life.

Self-help literature is likely to give more stress to you. Self-help will just get you lost in your thoughts. Self-help will get you stuck in your head. And that's why self-help is often no help at all. Be proactive and reactive. It should go without saying to be proactive in life, that's basically what helping yourself is all about. Start doing things that will benefit you. But you also need to be reactive to life.

I'm not saying to be reactive to your problems but, of course, you should react to and handle your problems before they get worse. What I'm saying is to be reactive when you see a problem coming. We all come across problems, that's what life is all about. But those who see a problem coming and react to it before it is a problem, they help themselves, are always better off. And being in the moment will help you to be proactive in life as you aren't wasting your time and energy in your fantasy worlds and will help you to be reactive to things as you're giving your full attention to what's going on in the real word. Then all that's required for you to do is to act, to help yourself.

First things first. There are actions that are certainly more important than others or at least bear more fruit. So the popular self-help advice of first things first does have merit. But that's why it's so important to know your real motivation in life and to keep a reminder close by. Make sure the actions you do that day move you towards that big dream of yours. And make sure that it is the first thing you do that day so you don't have an excuse at the end of the day that you ran out of time. Put first things first. I'll show later that your most important action will have something to do with other people and building relationships. If you don't know what your true motivation in life is, action and reflection will reveal it. Just more reason to focus on taking action. Just more reason to help yourself. Best way to build a healthy self-image. Some self-help books will tell you about the importance of a healthy self- image, mindsets, positive thoughts, etc.

Those things are good, not really great though, as they can help to make you feel good about yourself and that can motivate you to take action. But I have an even better way to build a good self-image, just take action! When you take action you'll know, not just simply think, that you can help yourself. It's the best way to break out of learned helplessness. Take enough action and you will come across some success eventually. Now you'll know that you can be successful. Take enough action and you'll start getting better at whatever it is that you do and success will come. Now you'll know that you are a success.

Knowing and thinking are worlds apart when it comes to having a healthy self-image. Focus too much on thinking ups a positive self-image or thinking about self-help positivity in general but there is a good chance you won't take action or not enough action to really make a difference in your self- image. Focus on action and let the rest take care of itself. While you can't take non-stop action since you are not a robot, living in the real world will force you to take action. But living in a fantasy world will distract you from taking action. And think about it, isn't thinking up a positive self-image is living in a fantasy world? Work in the real world. Take action. Sure, we all suffer from an unhealthy self-image from time to time and it can hinder you from taking action. But it can't stop you unless you let it stop you. And taking action, even if you have to start small and even if you have to start when you don't feel like it, will break you out of that rut.

Reading self-help and practicing positivity, however, will probably just keep you stuck in your head. Help yourself. Start taking action towards a better self-image. Be yourself I've already talked about this somewhat, but I want to cover it again: the truth is what works for one person won't necessarily work for you. What works for you won't necessarily work for someone else. We're all unique individuals.

And what works for you needs to be learned through you, through your experiences. Besides, when you're being your authentic self, instead of doing some self-help garbage, you'll feel a lot better about life. Sure, being honest with yourself will help you to be yourself, but, ultimately, knowing yourself has to come from experience, from interacting with the world, from helping yourself.

Will you make mistakes? Of course. Will it hurt? Yes sometimes. But everyone makes mistakes. What matters is whether you learn from them or not. Whether you hide in your room and mope about things or if you get out there and try again but this time a little wiser makes all the difference in the world. But part of being yourself is not blindly listening to self-help books. You are a unique individual with your own feelings. Start listening to them. They're telling you who you really are. So don't do things that don't feel right. Don't do things just because a self-help book told you to do them. Facing your fears is one thing, but if something doesn't feel right, it's probably best to listen to that feeling. So don't be afraid of new experiences, but do take the time to figure out if they're right for you. Listen to and accept your feelings on the subject. And the more experiences you get, the more feelings you'll tap into, and the more you'll start to discover who you really are.

Besides, the truth is every day is a self-improvement day, every day you learn something new to better your life. You don't need to be turning to self-help books. But how much you learn really depends on how much action you take, how much you help yourself. You learn the most about yourself from interacting with the world, not from reading someone else's thoughts. Be yourself and see what works for you. Just start at any time you can grab life by the horns and start steering it in the right direction. If there is something you don't like about your life, then change it. You don't have to wait for anyone's permission. If something is bothering you, then do something about it. But, if you procrastinate on things, then it'll just leave you in a worse situation. So don't be putting things off. It'll hurt you if you do. And if that's the case, then it's important to realize that consuming self-help is most likely just going to keep you from taking action.

Just start. Don't wait for that perfect moment.

Actually, try to aim for imperfect as it'll help you start. You could even aim for terrible or even the worst possible approach as it'll get you to begin and, surprisingly or unsurprisingly, if you know how the world really works, it'll often give you good results or at least show you what you should be doing instead. So don't get too stuck in your head trying to be perfect or trying to find that perfect moment. Just begin. Even if you fail, it'll help you to start to get over your fear and it'll help you figure out what to do next as you learn from your mistakes. But reading self-help, pondering theory, or doing nothing will just have the opposite effect.

Fear will start to grow, you won't really learn anything, and you'll get more confused on what to do for yourself. So it's better to try and fail than to waste your time reading self-help. As I said, when you start helping yourself, you will succeed and you will fail. The problem that comes is that you often completely fail at first or you quickly hit a threshold of success. And when that happens, when people feel trapped again, they run back to self-help. But that doesn't work. But neither will only helping yourself. Taking action in life is not enough. Like I said, you'll always be improving by taking action, but that won't improve your life fast enough in the limited amount of time you have. Helping yourself is critical. It's a required first step every time. That's why you should just start something instead of thinking about it. But taking action by yourself is never enough. There is only one way to get the results you want and it isn't self-help trash.

If you want to break free you have to ask for help. This is the most important part of the book by far as self-help tries to get you to rely on yourself, a bad strategy at best. But if you do this part of the book, you won't need self-help anymore. While the last step, giving help to others, is crucial to your happiness, there's a good chance you'll do it anyway, the more you interact with people and constantly asking for help will get you interacting with them. As for the first step, helping yourself often means asking for help. And that's usually the best way to help yourself in any situation. If you only apply one thing from this book, if you only take one action with it, let it be this. Why? Because the only way you can break free, the only way to get the results you really want in life, is with the help of others. But they aren't going to give it to you without asking as no one can read your mind. Right. You have to ask! You have to help yourself first. Most of your problems in life came from trying to do life entirely by yourself. By asking for help, it is forcing you to interact with the real world. It's forcing you to stop living in your own little self-help world. It's forcing you to be social. And when you're social, your problems and your life are no longer just your own. Going it alone, only focusing on the first step, will result in bad and/or unproductive action. You'll just get frustrated. You need people.

Remember being a loner is a killer of the dreams.

If taking action, (helping yourself) isn't giving you the results you want in life, that's because you haven't been asking people for help. Don't live life by yourself alone. What determines if you fail or succeed in life most often comes down to whether you are willing to ask for help or not. Yes, life really is that simple. Now I'm not talking about asking someone for help with your homework (but if you do need help with your homework, certainly, go ahead and ask). What I'm telling you is to ask for help with the things you want, most out of life sometimes all you really need is the emotional support, but you do need the emotional support. Yes, it'll take being honest with yourself to know what to ask, but it isn't really that hard to figure out.

The hard part is being willing to ask. Why? Because our dreams often seem too big to be accomplished. So it creates fear in us that we often justify as being something else like a sudden loss of interest, telling yourself you don't deserve it, or some other silly reason. These huge dreams of ours will certainly be a burden on anyone we ask, so why ask? But there is this incredible synergy created when we ask that it would be foolish not to ask since people love to help. And, surprisingly, they can be rather easy to accomplish, even the big ones, when you get the help of others. And the bigger the dream the more likely people will want to help. Asking for help is so underrated. And keeping your dream a secret will often kill it faster than anything else.

Just keeping secrets in general will tend to do you more harm than good. You need to open up to people. You need to ask them for help. But don't feel bad for asking. You're a human being. You need help. And you deserve to be helped. Everyone else got to where they are with the help of others, don't you deserve the same. And the great news is there are a tons of people out there who are willing to help you. All you have to do is ask. All you have to do is help yourself.

And I know you might feel greedy or selfish asking for help, but people love to help. It's in our nature. It makes us feel good. Why shouldn't you give them the opportunity to feel good about themselves? However, I know you might also be hesitant to ask for help because you don't know how to ask or who to ask, so I'll deal with that right now. Who to ask for help? Anyone and everyone, more the merrier. The more people who know that you need help, the more likely you'll get it. Of course, there are always exceptions to the rule.

There are certainly people who you should never ask for help. Who are they? I don't have to tell you. There is a reason why we tell kids to not talk to strangers. But you're an adult. You know who to ask, stranger or otherwise. But don't get me wrong, you will make mistakes. You will ask the wrong person for help, only slightly wrong as I'm quite sure I don't have to worry about you asking a deranged person for help, but you'll learn from it and you'll get better. So how do you ask? How to ask for help. It's pretty much the same idea as I just mentioned, the more you ask the better you'll get at it. So I would say focus more on asking (focus on taking action) rather than asking the perfect way. The latter will just get you stuck in your head and you should know by now how bad getting stuck in your head is for you. Remember, if you're having a hard time finding the courage to ask, try asking poorly or even the worst way possible as it'll get you to start. However, I will give this piece of advice, the more you communicate the better are the results.

If you need help with something, tell them why you need help, what you've already done and what your current ideas are, who you've already talked to, where you've already gone for help, how they can help you, etc. It is said that when you tell someone your dream it's important for them to know what is keeping you from getting it then they'll be more likely to help out. The more they can understand where you're coming from, the more they can relate to you, the more likely they'll be willing to help and the better they'll be able to help. You can't overlook the importance of communication. You need to let people know what you want. You need to let people know what is on your mind. They can't know or help otherwise. And often that communication starts with you asking for help. There really isn't that much else to say other than you're probably not going to ask for help. You'll read this chapter and just move on. Even after you've finished this book, you might do something to help yourself, but you probably won't get around to asking for help as it's a much bigger psychological hurdle to climb. But if you don't, you won't make enough progress and you'll just escape to your own little worlds again.

You probably keep escaping from the real world, and why you have no one there that you're willing to ask for help, because you have no real friends. And most people naturally do the three steps, without being told about them, because they have friends. If you think about it, the main point of this book (one of them at least) really is to, instead of focusing on or reading self-help, take action and get help from your friends and the results in your life are going to be thousands of times better. Help yourself. Ask for help. But if you don't have friends, then your massive action should be about making them. Just keep in mind, making friends is a gradual process that can't be rushed. However, you can't make friends unless you first help yourself by communicating, by interacting with people. And most friendships start by asking someone for a favor. So start asking people for help and you'll start making more connections with others. And your life will start to fall into place.

So here is my advice to you, use a simple tally system. Again, this isn't so much a self-help system but rather a reminder. Put it somewhere you can easily see. You could even put it on the back of a piece of paper with the three steps that is in your wallet or purse. Mark it each time you ask someone for help with your dreams. And every time you feel stuck, hopeless, depressed, or frustrated in life, look at the tally system and see how many people you have asked for help. If the answer is no one or very few, then you have no right to complain or to be hopeless. You know what needs to be done to break free, so do it. Finding people to ask, I know, you probably will feel shaky about who and how to ask for help as it probably seems like I'm suggesting you talk to strangers on the street.

You might certainly do but I think that that would be a little too difficult and awkward for the average person.

Let me offer a little structure on asking. First, talk to those closest to you like your friends, your family, and your neighbors. You'll be less afraid to ask them and they're often easy to access, so you can quickly get this idea or problem off your mind and into the real world. If you don't, you'll be very likely to start overthinking your problem/question, get stuck in your head while it grows in your imagination, and end up asking no one. Then you can reach out to organizations and well-known people in the community. This one will take a little bit of courage, but often there is a group or person that can help with your specific problem.

Sometimes it'll cost you money. But even if you can't pay, you can usually still get some good information from them that'll help you out. Finally, you can ask for help from the people who just happen to be around you at the moment. This one will often take even more courage if you happen to be surrounded by strangers, and this is why I mention it as your last option but you'll be surprised at the wealth of information or just plain good ideas random people can provide you. Plus, strangers are often willing to help you in ways that the people you know wouldn't. I think it's a psychological thing. They want to know that if one day they need to ask a stranger for help that they'll get it. And by being the helping stranger this time it feels like they're making it so. Or maybe people just like to impress strangers with how much they can help. Who knows? But people love to help others anyway (that is evolutionary biology, primordial man had no mechanical means to help him so people helped each other and nature built it in our genes.), so don't overthink it or worry about it. The help of a stranger might be exactly what you need to break free.

But an often neglected way to find people to help you is to join an interest group that shares your ideas and values as it'll be a lot easier to ask like-minded people. Even if they don't share your dream or type of dream,it's probably better if you find a group that does, but that can be a rare thing, when you share the same interests in something with another person they'll be more willing to help you out. Basically, people are often more friendly and thus more helpful to those who they can relate to with a common interest.

There is another way to find people to ask for help called an Idea club. An Idea Club is where you get people together, especially those who don't know each other too well. Acquaintances, neighbors, strangers etc., remember, are often willing to help out more than you think and in ways people who know you, won't, These clubs are specifically to figure out how they can help each other to fulfil their dreams.

Call up some people to come to your house and figure out together how to make each other's dreams come true. You can call it social networking (You can even make it a lunch or a dinner as an incentive for them to show up). Plus, you'll all feel great about helping each other out. And there probably are some other unique opportunities you alone have in your life for you to get people together to ask for help. So I would challenge you to come up with your own ideas. But, remember, the most important thing is to keep asking people for help. The more you ask the better you'll get at it, the easier it'll be for you to ask, and the more likely you'll get what you want.

Finally, don't forget to help yourself. Helping yourself is the first step. And the good thing about helping yourself is the fact that people will be more willing to help you if they see you already helping yourself, if they see you putting in the work. That's just human nature. That's why it's always a good idea to do the steps in order. Remember, you're never too old, too wise, or too experienced to ask for help. So don't let your pride or ego keep you from asking. We all need help in getting what we want from life. While asking for help will get you what you want, you might not be happy when you finally get it. That's where the last step comes in. So help yourself, ask for help, and that brings me to the last thing.

I'm going to break here and address those who have been reading self-help for years. There's probably something really off about your life and it's probably time to get some professional help. When it comes to people who read too much self-help, I think there are two groups: those who read it to escape boring, empty lives, who often never ask people for help or never talk to people about their problems like they should, and those who have suffered real trauma. While the latter definitely needs to see a professional, I think both groups would benefit from talking to someone about their dysfunctional life and a professional is your best bet. You might have to go through a few before you find one that clicks, but you really need to talk to someone if that's how your life is right now. Ask for help.

Give Help to others. If you think this is just about giving back to the world for all the help you've gotten, it's not. In fact asking for help actually has a lot to do with helping others as it allows them the enjoyment of helping you, to break free from their old routine. Helping others has a lot to do with helping yourself. When you give it, it creates this abundance to your life. It's hard to explain, but those who focus on giving end up getting even more back. You might not get money, but you'll get more than you ever need. Not that you should necessarily give just to get things back, rather it should be unconditional giving. In other words, you give simply to give. But cultivating that giving attitude takes practice. And I think it's a lot easier to want to give by getting first. When you have a lot in life (again, not just necessarily money or material goods) or when you feel fortunate for having something you naturally want to give back, even if it is out of guilt.

Again, that's why it's best to do the three steps in that order (at least when starting out) as it'll put you in the mood and create the opportunity to give. And you have to cultivate this giving mindset (even though I do believe it is in our nature to give) as we've been taught by society to be selfish individuals who don't care about other people's feelings and desires. But it's so important to practice giving as real happiness only comes from giving to others. Giving is also the fastest way to make friends, the fastest way to make sure you aren't doing life all by yourself and that's probably what caused you to turn to self-help in the first place. Sure, asking for help will probably help you make friends. Right communication will just about always improve a situation. But when you are giving to people (not just material goods, but compliments, kindness, resources, etc.), when you are of service to others, they'll want to be your friend. In short, if you want a friend, be a friend (be friendly to others).

And you typically have to give before you receive, so leading with giving can often be the best thing to do. So help yourself by giving to others. Some may say you are best just doing the last step. That is, focus on helping others and forget about your own desires. Putting the focus entirely on others will probably and anyway benefit your life. But that's something you will have to experiment with on your own. And isn't that what we're all here for, to serve others? But as much as we all want to believe in this sacred, unconditional loving connection to all of humankind, there's still the individual need to make things happen for ourselves, to be responsible for our own lives, to pull yourself up by your bootstraps, even if you just need to do it a little bit.

Again, and I know I keep repeating myself here, that's why I suggest you do the steps in order. You help yourself first, then you ask for help, and, finally, you give back to others. But how do you give? I don't think anyone can tell you that. Helping yourself and asking for help is pretty straightforward (they mostly just require you to face your fear). But giving is more of an art you develop over time and you can only develop that art if you practice it. Giving involves not only knowing yourself but also knowing the needs of those around you. You can always ask them (communication will always improve a situation), but people often don't even know what they really want or what will make them happy, that's why it's important for you to reflect on life, to be honest with yourself, and to keep trying new things as they allow you to know what will make you happy in life. It goes back to everyone being a unique individual though they don't always know themselves that well and also there being so many ways to give. You can give to charity or directly to the homeless. You can give your time to your friends or to a fatherless kid who needs guidance.

You can give an unexpected gift to a coworker or take them out to lunch. You can give your experience or just moral support even if one is paralyzed from the neck down, one can always give words of encouragement and that's often the best gift of all. What you can give is the best, what makes you feel the best when you give it, and how best to give it is up to you to find out. And you can only figure it out by trying things out, not *reading* about them. And it's so important to figure out how you can give back as it's the only way to true fulfilment. Listen to your feelings. But as much as we're all unique individuals, we're all still human. As such, we all want to feel appreciated. So sometimes the act of giving itself, even if you have no idea what they really want, is all that people want to receive.

So just focus on giving. Don't worry about doing it perfectly. However, I will offer a little bit of advice when it comes to giving to help you along. First, don't confuse helping others with pushing your values on people. People should be free to choose their own values in life. In other words, don't try to change people. Trust me, you'll be wasting your time. Instead, you should honor their individuality (find out what makes them happy). Next, don't help people who don't want to be helped. Again, people have the right to freedom and that freedom includes the choice to be helped or not. And you have no right to take that away from them. Also, don't let people dictate your life. Giving doesn't mean you do what people tell you to do. To really give you have to be happy first and that involves loving yourself. And if you love yourself, you'll communicate when things don't feel right. Finally, don't be a martyr. Don't kill yourself trying to help people and don't help people who bring you down.

Some individuals will hate you for no other reason than you're a person that they can hate. And they're free to do that. But you're also free to not waste your time with them. You'll do a lot more good in this world if you work with people and do actions that lift you up. You don't have to give to everyone, you don't have to be a living saint and trying to be one probably goes against being true to yourself.

You should be nice to everyone, but you don't have to be looking like meddlers into everyone's lives. Instead, find people who you want to give to and who appreciate you giving the most. There are other people who can better help everyone else. Remember, we're all unique individuals. Find your community. I know that seems like a lot to remember, but, honestly, you'll just have to figure it out first hand from experience. I'm just giving you this information so you'll hopefully connect the dots sooner as you learn through adversity, same for all of this book. However, you can only really understand what is said in this book by doing the three steps, by taking action. Help yourself.

Like I said, giving to others is a bit of an art, so you

have to practice it. But you will get good at it if you practice. If you do end up reading a lot of self-help after this book (or maybe you've already read tons of it)one thing you'll notice echoed over and over is the importance of other people in all aspects of your life like your career or business, your health, your happiness, and so on. The power of association and whatnot. But instead of reading about it, why don't you just live it. Put the focus on making other people happy and being around those you love. Give to them. But you have to be the one to make that effort to get that kind of life.

You have to put yourself out there, ask for help, and help others. And if you have read a lot of self-help, it's probably best to just forget about it all. That might be hard for some of you as you'll have to accept it was a waste of time, but that really is the best thing you can do. Not only will thinking about all that stuff probably get you stuck in your head, but it's best to face your current situation with a fresh mind and your full attention. And just like getting rid of a lot of material goods you don't need, you'll feel better once you get all that junk out of your head and house. And when you focus on giving people what they want, doing what will make them happy, they will want to be around you. People like to feel good, and if you can give that to them, they'll want to be with you. But again, you have to make the effort. You need people.

That's why it's best to put your focus on them instead of self-help. And giving is also how you make a living. People only hand you money after you give them a product, a service, or a promise of such. So giving is how you get rich (it's obviously not the only way but definitely the best in regards to your happiness). Making money is all about finding out what people want and giving it to them. Communicate. The more you can give and the more it meets other people's desires, the more you'll get back. But, again, what you are best suited for when it comes to contributing the most to the world and in return receiving the most back and as I keep saying, not necessarily money but happiness can only be learned through experience and experimenting and a fat bit of communication. It'll probably have something to do with one of your strengths. But how to best apply that strength to the real world has to come from experience, not from reading business books/self-help.

Let the real world teach you what it wants you to give. And if you're broke, make another tally list and start tracking the number of people you've helped get what they really wanted out of life. If the number is zero, then you know why you're broke but then you also know what needs to be done. There is one last thing I want to leave you with. There is something that could be better than the three steps. It's to just do what you enjoy. Because what you really enjoy if you're being completely honest with your self is spending time with those you love. And as long as you communicate, you'll naturally help each other out and push each other forward, you'll naturally do the three steps so you could change your three steps to just communicate, be social, to just keep putting yourself out there with people, or whatever works for you. Being with others is what will allow you to get the most of what you want from life. It'll make you happy, so why wouldn't you do it? And that covers all three of the steps. But we're not done yet because I know there's a good chance you'll go back to self-help anyway. So let me spoil all those "great" self-help ideas there are so you don't waste your time and energy. Let's talk about all that bad self-help out there waiting to trip you up.

Bad self-help ideas won't get you unstuck. If you aren't miserable, perhaps you're just stuck in life but if you're stuck, trust me, you're miserable, you've just numbed yourself to it with different comforts. The answer isn't self-help but doing something to improve your situation. Even if you can only improve it a little bit, you can then improve that new, slightly better situation a little bit more. Then you repeat that, again and again. You just have to help yourself. Don't let your feelings of apathy or fear keep you from taking action. Don't run to self-help as an easy way to feel better about your situation. And if apathy or fear is the reason you fail to take action, running back to self- help is the worst thing you can do. I know you think you'll find something that will help or accelerate your progress towards facing your fears or getting what you want from life, but it won't.

Only other people can really accelerate your progress and that's about it. And you'll probably need them anyway to break free. Tell people what you want from life. That's how you get it. So don't be afraid to tell people your desires. Ask people for help. By not taking action, by staying in your room reading self-help, your fear, apathy, and loneliness will just grow. You're making the situation worse. You just have to face your fears. I know those books have little tricks in them, like affirmations or whatever, to try to help. But, in my opinion, even if they do some good, you'll probably just get stuck back in your head again, you'll get stuck back in your own little self-help world. Why risk trapping yourself again? Instead of doing something that might work to help you face your fears, do the thing that you know that will work to help you face your fears. I can guarantee facing your fears, or even trying to face your fears, will improve things. It might not seem like it at first, it might seem like you're just spinning your wheels, but if you keep at it, you will see results.

So forget those tips and tricks and just do what needs to be done.

The only real benefit I can see from self-help is to offer you some guidance in the right direction. That's why this book. But you can get that same guidance from good people you know. And the right direction in life is genuine connection with others, not fake ones. Isolation is what caused you to get stuck. And self-help is what's perpetuating your isolation. Stop trying to do it all alone and reach out for help. Ask for help. Even when you do get what you want from life, even if you do get unstuck from your current situation, you might get stuck with an empty feeling inside. But I can guarantee fulfilment if you help other people. Give help to others. The three steps will give you what you really want in life, they'll help you get unstuck, but how you apply the three steps is up to you to figure out.

There is no *Secret* in self-help (And It Won't Help you With Your Fears) I wish there was some secret to getting what you want in life, but there's not. Law of attraction is no secret. You just have to put in the work. And I wish there was some secret to getting over your fears, but you just have to keep trying until you do. But if there is some strategy that works well for you, you're probably going to have to learn it on your own. And you learn things by trying stuff out. Help yourself. For the most part, life is all about figuring things out for yourself. But you can figure things out. You can blaze your own trail. You can have an amazing life. Of course, you'll have your good days and your bad days. You'll have days where you feel like you made amazing progress, but most of the days you'll feel like you made none or that you even went in reverse.

But you are making steady progress, even if it doesn't feel like it at times. So keep at it.In fact, strategic breaks can help you improve faster but not if you let them break your consistency. So keep trying new things, keep putting yourself out there. You'll figure it out. But you won't get there sticking to your old habits, staying in your room, and doing the same thing each day. You won't get there if you keep reading self-help. You won't get there if you don't face your fears. And you get over your fear by keeping at it, by chipping away at it little by little. Running back to self-help will just halt or even reverse your progress.

You just have to keep trying, keep pushing forward as you will get somewhere but only if you try. Again, it can be easy to run back to your self-help books thinking, or hoping, you'll find some secret answer. But, and I can't say this enough, there is no secret. You just have to start working to get unstuck. You have to start working to get the life you want. Help yourself. And, like I said, if you really want to accelerate your progress towards being successful or facing your fears (and maybe this is the secret you've been looking for) only other people and your community can really push you forward in that regard. We are a social species. But they won't help if you don't ask. Ask for help. Besides, what you really want is happiness, not success. However, working with and being around the right people will bring you both. The feeling of being stuck, actually being stuck, and not getting what you desire in life has a lot to do with the people you surround yourself with. They lack resources or intelligence, they annoy you, they don't understand you, they're not willing to help, and/or they drag you down.

Well, guess what? There are plenty of fish in the sea. You can have your own group of people you love. But it's up to you to find them. You just have to ask people for help. You have to help yourself. You have to go after the life you want. Like I said, you can ask strangers for help. Strangers are new people with new possibilities for you. But going to some activity you like where you can meet new people with something in common is probably your best bet. You don't have to put up with those who you grew up with. You don't have to put up with bad people. But you do need to find the courage to stop living how you've been living and help yourself. There is no secret in self-help. You just need to find the courage to put yourself out there.

Grit Is the ticket to misery and failure. Strange isn't. Does grit work? But it's not going to give you what you really want in life. In fact, it's going to leave a really bad taste in your mouth. Perseverance always works. And grit is the type of perseverance where you stick to it even when it hurts. To me, that's not the best way to get things done. If you did ten years at a job with your friends who you loved spending your time with, would you say that you had perseverance? Of course, you did it for ten years straight. Now would you say you had grit? No, you always enjoyed going to work each day and you only went to work because you enjoyed being with your friends. So you don't have to use grit to accomplish big things. Whatever you're aiming for, give it enough time and you'll get it. But you only have so much time in life, which means you can only aim for so many things and get them. So what are you aiming for? Are you aiming for the right things? Too often, people use grit to go after the wrong things in life. Grit is good if you use it for right things.

Besides, it's not the destination that matters, it's the journey. And if you're using a ton of grit in life (sometimes it is necessary or best for you to use a little bit of grit here and there) but how can you possibly enjoy the journey? You just have to learn to relax and enjoy the adventure that is life. Don't be so serious. Don't be so demanding of yourself all the time. Life is meant to be enjoyed. While grit might get you success, praise, worldly pleasures, and even a lot of cash, things like that won't give you self actualization.

But you can get those things a lot faster and easier by working with others. After making all those sacrifices and doing all that hard work to find nothing at the end, it'll leave you miserable. While grit will get you what you want, it'll fail at giving you what you need. And that is the difference And what you need are some friends. What you need is to enjoy your life while you have it. What you need is to be honest with yourself. Forget the grit; focus on being who you really are. Stop trying so hard and let things be. Sometimes let go. To be fair, what I call perseverance others might call grit. The main point is to be able to enjoy life for the most part while you're alive. And, especially, don't make yourself miserable for things you really don't care about. And I'm not against using grit to make your dreams come true as long as it's something you do without thinking about it because it means that much to you. Like I said before, be true to yourself.

Being a Salesman isn't the answer. I know a lot of people who think so and self-help books will tell your life is just a numbers game. Just do it enough times and you'll see results. Even with this book, I know you're thinking," man if I help myself as much as I can, ask enough people for help, and give help to a mountains of other people, I'll have anything I want and a wonderful life!" While that's true, you're not a robot. A numbers game will drain you mentally and physically. It's not natural.

Remember, grit isn't how you want to live your life. But isn't life a numbers game? To a certain extent, absolutely. But if you live your life that way you won't be happy and I guarantee you'll be a lot less productive than you think. With the three steps and me telling you to keep doing them is really about changing how you approach life. So it's really not about doing the three steps as much as possible; it's about training yourself to not suffer in silence, to communicate more with others, to ask for help when you need it, and to start focusing on others and building relationships. It's about learning how to be a good person who is connected to others, not using people or making yourself into a robot.

Yes, you can aim for a certain number each day if you want, but view it as a daily workout. While I'm against planning alone as you'll read about later, making yourself miserable in obtaining your dreams, and trying to force habits is not my take. I am not against setting specific daily goals (I'm not necessarily for it either) as long as they serve to keep you on track to develop you as person, to improve your relationships, to help you focus on your dreams, and to focus on others. While there is a Zen-like quality to this book, you'll still need some self-discipline and focus to make sure you're putting the most important things in life first. You work out your muscles in the gym and, here, I'm getting you to work out your personality at home. And a workout has to come to an end and you have to recover for a period for it to do any good. But you also have to be consistent at it for it to work.

So put in the work each day. Even if you have to start with very light weights and you'll see the results in time. But overdo it and you'll just get burnt out or injured. Just start by doing a bit of the three steps today. Help yourself or ask someone for help. And then try to do a little bit more each day after that. Before you know it, it'll be part of your personality and you'll start getting results. I would suggest you start by looking at your piece of paper each morning or at night planning for the day ahead and ask yourself what is one thing you can do to help yourself, something you can ask someone for help with, and one way you can give to others for this day. Try to aim as small as possible. While it might not feel like you are doing much, not only are you ingraining the steps into your personality but those little actions will add up to make a big difference. Start small. Start slow. But do start. And don't stop.

However, and I can't emphasize this enough, don't stress when it comes to the three steps. Just slowly start to incorporate them into your life. I know this sort of thing goes against the tally system I gave you earlier in the book, but I gave it as it's better to do too much of the three steps than not doing them at all. It's more of a reminder than anything else, another one as you can't really be reminded enough, to start doing the steps. However, the best thing you can do is to naturally include them into your life. *But just blindly doing the three steps as much as you can* is no different than just following what those self-help books say. Will you get some results? Yes, but you'll burn out and get tired of it. Then you'll move on to the next self-help technique you find interesting.

Be true to yourself instead. Do what feels right. Slowly growing and maturing as a person, learning to gradually incorporate the three steps into your life, will feel right. Don't be a salesman like all those self-help books tell you to do. Don't treat people or life like a numbers game. Instead, be true to yourself. Most people who have tried being a salesman at some point in their lives will tell you how hard and fruitless of a job it was for them. While there are certainly salesmen in this world who can make a living at it, the most successful salespeople I see will tell you it isn't a numbers game. They'll tell you it's about building relationships and helping people get what they want. And that's what life is all about.

Writing down a plan is often planning to fail. No, I have nothing against planning and I find it beneficial, helpful, and even necessary at times. I'm just against how the vast majority of people plan when it comes to their ideal life. Too often, the way they plan guarantees they will fail in achieving it. Don't get me wrong, you do have to plan for life. Failing to plan is planning to fail. And I think writing things down can serve as a great reminder, that's why I had you write down the three steps. But don't try creating some type of secret treasure map, some ultimate plan that will lead you to the promised land. Doing something like that isn't good for you (at least not when you do it alone). It goes back to the idea of taking action and not being stuck in your head imagining these fantasy worlds.

Besides, I can guarantee those long-term plans you come up with on your own won't work out,at least not the way you expect them to, which means they're ultimately a waste of your time. Instead, take advantage of your current opportunities. Planning and scheduling for the short-term, the next day, week, or even month, is mandatory in a life where you work but don't forget to plan for the fun activities you want to do as well. And having a wish or a dream written down is a good way to keep yourself from drifting in life or wasting time on unimportant things. And adding that dream to your piece of paper with the three steps wouldn't be such a bad idea. But too often planning the details for that dream turns into you living in a pleasure island as deep down inside, you'll think it's too big of a dream that you'll never have and that all you can really do is fantasize about it. When you plan alone things will seem impossibly big. Plus, planning for what is in between your short-term planning and your ultimate wish is almost impossible as life will never unfold the way you expect it. It becomes a waste of time. Especially, and you'll notice I'll keep saying this again and again, if you plan alone.

Actually, the only exception to the rule of over planning being harmful is planning with others as they'll keep you accountable, keep you in the real world, and as a group they can effectively fill in a lot of the in- between areas through their vast experiences and knowledge. But when you plan with other people you don't have to write it down, though you certainly can and you probably will have to write some items down in a schedule so you don't forget them. The most important thing is that you keep communicating about your plans with others. As long as you keep an open dialogue with others about what is going on in your life with your hopes and dreams you'll do just fine.

But since it's our personal fantasies we're talking about here, we too often plan alone out of embarrassment. You have to get over that. Besides, planning with people and letting people help with your plans is taking advantage of your current opportunities. So, yes, get in the habit of scheduling your life so you show up on time and so you won't forget appointments. And, no, there is no best or secret technique for scheduling you'll find in a self-help book. You just have to keep doing it as you'll get better over time and figure out what works for you. And after you've reflected on life, you should be able to, and you should for the sake of clarity, write down what really matters the most to you, what you really want out of life, and keep it close by. But after that, you need to start talking to people, you need to start asking for help. Don't plan anything on your own. It's just too risky you'll get caught up in your head in a fantasy world instead of taking action. Planning like that will cause you to fail.

If you do want to write down a plan, do it with people. Plus, planning with others also gives you the opportunity to give, to help other people make their dreams come true. That means if you're willing to help yourself by getting a group together, you get to do all the three steps in one. Again, nothing wrong with planning. But if you let planning or researching a topic by yourself take you off to this fantasy world where you do nothing with it (as the vast majority of people do) you're planning to fail. But every time you take action in the real world, when you help yourself, the best course of action will start to emerge and it'll be clear what you need to do next. And then you don't have to worry about perfecting your plans. But you won't find that out hiding in your room researching and plotting. You need to live in the real world with real people.

And by interacting with real people, you're much more likely to get what you want from life. In other words, take action, help yourself, and learn if it's a good action or plan, see what the results are. And if that process is taking too long to get you what you want, start getting other people involved. Ask for help. So if you just focus on taking action and getting help when you need it, there really is no need to plan. Or, rather, the right plan will start to emerge on its own when you start taking action and communicating with others about what you want. Besides, there's no guarantee when you get what you want, that secret fantasy of yours that it'll make you happy. So writing down a master plan by yourself and applying grit to it is probably not the best idea in the world as you'll be miserable as you pursue it and could be miserable once you get it.

It's better to enjoy the journey called life while you go after what you want. And when you do things with others, like letting them help you with your dreams, it becomes a lot easier to enjoy the journey. Even if you do accomplish your dream by yourself, other people hold the key to your personal development, so you can see why doing self-help by yourself or just being alone in general, more often than not results in stunted growth. But you don't always need a dream, sometimes a dream can find you. Instead of reflecting on things too much trying to figure out what to do, see what the world has to offer.

Take action. In other words, let life show you the way. Instead of trying to create your plans alone for a big dream you'll probably never do, or that'll leave you empty inside once you get it, take advantage of your current opportunities in the real world, that also means don't be planning to redo your past. Use the moment you have right now. And your opportunities right now in the real world involve people one way or another. And those current opportunities will evolve into big life plans that will give you the fulfilment you are looking for. They'll give you fulfilment, or at least be far more likely to give you fulfilment, as you can learn and tweak your plans from what the real world teaches you as you go along unlike those plans you are making in the dark. It's much better strategy than getting stuck in your head planning for your fantasy future or wasting all your time alone on a big project that doesn't pan out.

When you plan alone in secret, it's because deep down you're assuming the Universe, God, or whatever you believe in is against you. The Universe really cares about you and wants to help you, at least the vast majority of the people who live in it do. That means you just need to start turning to people for help with your dreams. And if those close to you can't help, or can't help enough, then start turning to other people until you find those who can. Trust me, the world is an amazing place with amazing possibilities. You just have to start interacting with it, you have to put yourself out there, and you have to communicate with people. And that's the answer you're looking for to get unstuck. That's the secret to accomplishing amazing things. Plan with people, ask them for help with your dreams. Don't try to go it alone.

Chasing after success will leave you miserable. Habits are bad News. I've sort of already touched on this topic with grit: chasing after success is a recipe for disaster. You should be chasing after better friendships and family life. Remember, put the focus on others. You don't want to be that person who has a well-paying job but no friends or family of your own. Like I said before, you will get what you aim for, but it doesn't mean you'll be happy when you get it. And when it comes to habits, is that really what you want to become, a robot? Even if you can take grit and pain out of the equation, you're still chasing after success. With the limited time you have, that means you're giving up other very important things to get it. Don't get me wrong, there is a time for work and there is a time for play. Sometimes you have to buckle down to do what needs to be done. And if you want to space things out, that's fine and a lot of times that's the smart thing to do. But don't let it turn you into a soulless robot, that's no way to live.

Remember, all you have is the present moment. Don't waste it. You don't have to prove anything to anyone. Life just needs to be enjoyed. It's not a competition. You just need to start being true to yourself. You need to start enjoying the journey. Besides, like I said, if you are going to chase after something, it's a lot more enjoyable if you do it with others. Ask for help. And you can't really force habits; they're too ingrained. Habits tend to just naturally happen when you don't try. It is more enjoyable that way. Let things just come together when it's their time. Don't try to force habits. Don't chase after success. It'll just work when everything is ready.

Mentors are just unnecessary abuse. If you want to get a mentor, think twice about it changing your life for the better. A mentor needs to care for you to make any difference in your life. They first need to be your friend for them to work because it is really the emotional support that you need from them. But that emotional support can make all the difference in the world. Most of the stuff they are going to teach you are things you already know or can easily figure out on your own. That means in the self-help world mentorships are worthless, but friends who you can turn to are worth their weight in gold. You just have to ask them for their advice. Ask for help.

And if you need an accountability partner, no one will do a better job than your friend. They care enough to make the effort to keep you on track and they will provide the emotional support you need to accomplish your goals. Something like a sports coach would be different of course. That's skill and knowledge being passed down. Mentoring, however, or what some call life coaching, is often one person talking down to another or just trying to sound smarter. No good really comes from that. What you really want is a friend to talk to. You just have to ask them for help. And a friend will lift you up, not pull you down.

Tips and Tricks will Just Trip You Up. But there are always the tips and tricks that'll allure you to read self- help like that psychological technique that showed this percentage increase in success in this situation. It certainly seems like good stuff to know. But let me warn you, those tricks won't really help as they'll hurt you.Why not just be yourself? The truth catches up to you eventually and you can always improve any skill by just doing it. There's no need for tricks. What about using all those tips and tricks on yourself? Then you're just manipulating yourself from not being the person you're supposed to be. And how can you enjoy life if you aren't being who you really are? Again, why not be yourself? It's the only way to really live.

There are no shortcuts; you just have to put in the work. If you want to learn a new skill, just practice it until you get good at it. There is no other way. So don't waste your time reading self-help. Don't get me wrong, you'll figure out new strategies in life (or tricks if you want to call them that) that work for you, but those have to grow from time and experience. So just focus on taking action and you'll figure out the best path to take. Focus on doing the work. Ultimately, it all has to come from you. Be yourself. Don't be digging in those self-help books for those little golden nuggets. It's all just fool's gold. You just need to do what needs to be done. Personally, I find if you just be yourself though, oddly enough, you have to work at it, you have to take a lot of action,you naturally do all those tips and tricks without thinking about it but without the karma recoil or the bad taste in your mouth from trying to manipulate others.

Forget the tips and tricks. Be who you really are. Chasing after happiness is also a bad Idea.So you shouldn't chase after success. And just about everyone knows that chasing after happiness is also a foolish endeavor. There's a lot of evidence showing that the people who chase after happiness quickly become miserable. Now even self-help books are coming out saying to not chase after happiness. Then they tell you the trick is to setup your environment to make it more likely you'll be happy. But that's still chasing after happiness. The main problem with chasing after happiness is that you're still making yourself the focus in your life.

Remember, you're supposed to put the focus on others. Instead of chasing after happiness, what you should be doing each day is the right thing. Communicate with people, donate your time and money, put in the work to be of value to others, but ask for help when you need it, help out a friend, be a good person, etc. Our brains are wired to make happiness the reward for doing the right thing. And, trust me, it's not going to let you cheat. So stop turning to self-help looking for tricks to be happy. And how you get yourself into a good environment that will help to make you happy is by doing the right thing. Doing the right thing will slowly get you to a good, happy environment. That's because what is really going to make you happy is a sense of community (that's the best environment to have). But you get that sense of community by helping others by putting the focus on others, by doing the right thing.

So stop wasting your time reading self-help books to find happiness. Happiness comes from the right action. So start doing the right actions. Stop chasing after happiness and make your life about helping others. Focus on making other people happy. And you do that one person at a time by giving your undivided attention. You can't rush the process. That's also how you make friends. And making someone into a friend is also a gradual process. But that doesn't mean making friends is hard.

Actually, it isn't so much about making friends but finding friends. You can't make anyone do anything. You don't make opportunities; you find opportunities. Like Lord Hanuman found opportunity in Lord Ram's plight. There were millions of other monkeys there but Lord Hanuman took advantage of the opportunity and became famous for all time to come. You find your friends. But even when you find them it just takes time for not only them to trust you but for you to trust them. So just keep putting yourself out there and be friendly, give people your undivided attention. Never forget, deep down people just want to be seen and heard. And you have the power to give that. Give to others. Don't try to make yourself happy. Instead, focus on making other people happy. This isn't to say you shouldn't chase after your dreams. Just don't chase after the feeling of happiness. But do live out your dreams. People want to see that. Go after what you want from life. By living up to your full potential, doing what you're good at, what you enjoy, and what you really want from life, you're making society happy. Believe me, it's the best way to serve others.

Self-Help is Deadly.Have you ever met someone who was really into self-help and who wasn't off it? Yet, do you think when you're the one reading self-help you're not the one others are seeing as off? It's because you and the other people out there reading self-help think that there's some type of secret to be found to improve your life. There is not. And you have to be kind of off to think that. Normal people know that self-help is either garbage or, if it is good, it's just common sense or things you already know. So they don't waste their time with it.

They just focus on doing the work. They focus on achieving their goals. They focus on taking action.

Haven't you already been taught to help others, be social, communicate, be proactive, and be a good person? And what do you think this whole book has been about? The secret there is that there is no secret. But the more you read and use self-help the more you're going to think you need it because you aren't going to see any results since you aren't putting in the real work that needs to be done. And when you do see people getting results who don't read self-help, which makes sense since they are not only putting in the real work that needs to be done but they also have more time to do so by not reading self-help, you're just going to get depressed about it. Then you're going to run back to self-help even more or give up altogether. But there's a better option, that's just to live your life. It means getting a life and being with the people you love, not relying on some book to solve your problems. Helping yourself and getting help from others. Just put yourself out there with people and see what works for you. Don't get stuck in your head, it won't do you any good. It'll just hurt you.

You need to have faith in yourself and in your own abilities to solve your own problems. That's how life is meant to be lived. This doesn't mean you can't talk to people about your problems or that you have to face them alone. But books can't talk back nor can they think about your current circumstances. But people can. Ask for help. Besides, every day is a self-improvement day. Every day you learn something new about yourself, the world, or you learn a new strategy to make life better. But that stuff is best learned from your life, from taking action, not from burying your head in books with material that you may never use. Don't focus on self-improvement. Don't focus on fixing yourself. Instead, go after what you really want in life. And when you do that you should naturally do the three steps, which means you probably haven't been going after what you really wanted in life this whole time. You might ask, though I've already answered it.

"Do I focus on making other people happy or do I focus on going after what I really want in life?" The answer is both. You can juggle more than one ball at a time. And they feed into each other. When you make people happy, they'll be much more likely to help you with your dreams. When you accomplish your dreams, you'll make those closest to you happy. And what you really want, if you're being honest with yourself, is to connect, help, and be with people. You could focus entirely on making other people happy. Perhaps that's what your real dream is about. Go after your dreams. Help yourself. Don't do the three steps to fix yourself. Do the steps for a better life. Once you stop thinking you need to fix or improve yourself, once you accept yourself as you are, things will start to improve as you'll free up time and energy to do exactly that. Use the three steps to get what you really want from life, not to fix yourself.

Even if you do care about self-improvement, I guarantee, instead of reading self-help looking for new techniques, if you focus on taking action, creating your own systems and ways of thinking from experience, and being with the right people, your results will be far better. But if you keep reading self-help material, you're reinforcing this idea that you're inadequate, that you need to keep reading self-help, and that makes sure you do keep wasting your time. Getting lost in these thoughts and wasting your limited time on earth with this stuff all alone is what makes self-help so deadly to living the life you want. It's detrimental to your success. It's deadly to your happiness. It's deadly to your social life. And it'll probably leave you feeling dead inside.

That means turning to self-help might have been one of the worst decisions of your life. What if the more knowledge you gain through self-help, the more miserable you become. Then really the best thing you can do is to just act, take part of this game called life and stop educating yourself through books. Trust me, the nature wants you to figure it out on your own, it wants to teach you directly, it wants you to live your own adventure. The important thing, and this is rather cliché since all self-help books end on this note, is that you focus on taking action the right action at least and the right action involves other people.

Go and see what the universe has in store for you. Stop with your planning, your reading, and your hiding in your room. Stop trying to outsmart the natural laws.. You just need to throw yourself into it and let the Universe provide and teach you. It's waiting for you; all you have to do is start. Let go of self-help so you can start doing what needs to be done. And what needs to be done is to get a life (and following the three steps can help with that). Don't let self-help pull you down to a situation where you get stuck in your head and you don't take action, where you think you can't figure out your own problems, where you can't enjoy your life. Stay far away from self-improvement material. Treat self-help like the plague because it is what it is. Help yourself by letting go of self-help. Let go of it and be free.

Why Self-Help? I don't think many self-help books address why you came to self-help in the first place. Happy people don't read this stuff. So that must mean some type of misery caused you to come here. And, thus, you are trying to fix that misery. Let's talk about that misery. Most miseries don't come purely from life circumstances but, rather, dysfunction is often the real culprit. Most of the time true misery comes from a dysfunctional reaction to a bad or harsh life circumstance. Bad things happen to everyone. But most people learn to prevent, adapt, and remove themselves from bad situations. But dysfunctional people have bad life strategies which often cause them to make poor life choices. That is why they end up running to self-help material looking for new techniques to use. While not terrible, those techniques found in self-help books tend to be a poor fit and, ultimately, a waste of time for most.

Remember, we're all unique individuals with unique life circumstances. What works for one person probably won't work for you, at least not in the long-run. But normal, healthy people have their own good techniques and life strategies which they prefer and enjoy compared to everyone else's created through experience, not through self-help books. So that raises the question Are normal people just way smarter than the dysfunctional people who turn to self-help? Are they simply able to come up with better life strategies on their own? No, not really. The difference lies in the fact that normal people talk to those they trust (and who aren't dysfunctional themselves) about their current problems and opportunities. This review process (though they probably never think about it that way, they just call it talking about their day) gets them to learn about good strategies and techniques for their situation and gets them to throw away the bad ones. And it often gets them to consistently make good decisions which add up to a successful, happy life. Ask for help.

Through experience ie taking action/helping themselves and talking to people about their current life situation excommunicating/asking for help they end up way better off in life. And those dysfunctional people who distract themselves from taking action with escapism and who keep to themselves by keeping secrets often find that they are not even close to the life they wanted, even with self-help material. And it's only a matter of time before they end up becoming miserable. Isolation isn't just the dream killer, it's the person killer. It's the path to a terrible life. It'll destroy your happiness, your success, your relationships, your finances, and your social life. So stop trying to do life by yourself.

Stop wasting your time with self-help. Talk to someone about your problems. Go open up to some good people. Go get some help. But, unfortunately, for those who have been reading self-help for a while, most miseries are pretty entrenched into their lives. In other words, it's not going to be a quick fix. Even though many self-help books have already said that, though they often imply the opposite on their cover and marketing, you're still looking for that quick fix, that secret to transforming your life. If you have already consumed a lot of self-help, think of an average day in your life. Has self-help really changed your actions in your day- to-day life? Even if it has, have those new actions really changed your life for the better? Probably not.

Sure, perhaps you gained new insights while reading it, which made you feel good in the moment, but if it hasn't changed your day-to-day actions and your results, you've gained nothing. And where you are today is a culmination of your hard work and your right actions, and nothing else besides your starting circumstances. So if you aren't happy with where you are, get to work doing the right thing.

Don't waste your time reading self-help. Instead, go talk to someone about your problems. Focus on action. Focus on getting help from others. Ask for help.

Like I said, a lot of your misery probably came from (actually, I'm quite certain of it) doing life all by yourself. And self-help, especially if you are looking for new material to consume all the time, is causing you to keep trying to do life all by yourself. Just let it go and start asking people for help. Talk to people about your problems. I guarantee there's no secret in those self-help books and there's no secret out there no matter where you look. The only secret in the self-help world is that they want you to get stuck in your head, they want you to think life is harder than it really is, so that way you end up wasting your time, energy, and, ultimately, your money on them. Everything has already been said before in one shape or another. The "secret" is to actually live your life and get help from others. Help yourself and get some help. And once you're in good shape, then you can start giving back and your life will get even better.

Now some of you might have turned to self-help looking for some ultimate truth to the universe or to the nature of life itself. Though, if you're being honest with yourself, you're probably looking for something outside yourself to justify your misery. Unfortunately, there could be no ultimate meaning to the universe or to life itself; however, your life does have meaning to it as it is a subjective experience. But how you discover that meaning has to ultimately come from you. Meaning is something unique to the individual. Thus, the only way to find it isn't through someone else's thoughts but through living your life, through helping yourself. One other thing to consider, focusing on your misery is what's probably perpetuating your misery. That is, telling yourself that you're broken inside or hopeless is what's causing you to be even more miserable and making it hard to act. And reading self-help is just reinforcing that.

Instead, if you shift your mindset, you'll do better. Instead of trying to fix yourself, focus on going after what you really want from life. Chase your dreams. But you don't have to be positive about it as everybody says. Actually, you should admit to yourself that you're feeling negative emotions as that'll free up your thoughts and energy to do something about it. Just don't dwell on those negative emotions and don't use them as an excuse. Acknowledge them, be okay with them, and move on. You can't let your emotions dictate your life so don't be waiting for the positive ones, and often you have to act in spite of them. Remind yourself of what really motivates you, what you really want from life like I already suggested, I would add it to your three steps. Bad things will have a tendency to just bounce off of you when you are chasing after your dreams. But the main point is to stop beating yourself up for no reason. If you do that all the time you'll never stop with the self-help. Take action instead. Help yourself and go after what you want from life.

This book talks a lot about putting the focus on others, but like I said you still have your own dreams, motivations, and feelings. You're a unique individual. Be who you are. Be yourself. Honor yourself. If you don't, it'll drain you. If you do, it'll energize you to better serve others. And, in turn, that'll help you get even more of what you want in life. While not a secret, I will say what might be considered a simple fix (definitely not an easy or quick fix though) is to stop thinking bad thoughts. Negative thoughts, considering what might go wrong, that you're feeling bad, or thinking of how you messed up, aren't always bad for you. But bad/evil thoughts, thinking of harming or hating others, yourself, or just selfish thoughts in general, will hurt you as they will lead to actions.

They might not lead to the exact actions you imagined, but they will lead to harmful actions and that is when karma or just how the real world works eventually gets you, and that's often when you go back to self-help. But you can also think of good thoughts, think of how thankful you are for everything you have, think of how you can give to others, and think of how much you love others, and those thoughts will lead to actions that will almost certainly do you good. And they'll help you get the life you desire. But you always knew those bad thoughts weren't good for you. So stop thinking bad thoughts.

Help yourself. Don't follow evil. All of its promises are just an illusion. Evil will just leave you worse off in the long run.

We all have evil within us, but it's up to each of us to not let it win. But if evil (your thoughts or otherwise) seems too overwhelming to overcome, just remember all evil comes from dysfunction/immaturity. And all dysfunctions and immaturities can be fixed. You don't defeat evil, you unravel it. That includes the evil in your own heart. But how you do that is for you to figure out, however, turning to an ally for help is always a good idea when facing true evil. Ask for help. But you don't have to kill yourself getting the life you want. Letting go of self-help doesn't have to be an epic battle of good versus evil.

You don't have to be a Zen master to have a good life. And taking action doesn't have to be hard on you. You have to stop being so serious about life and enjoy it and reading books on how to live your life is probably taking it a little bit too seriously. You'll just burn out doing that. You have to stop caring in a way. You have to stop trying so hard. Once you give up being so serious, you'll find even more energy and ability to go after what you really want. And if you're feeling really bad or depressed, it's probably best to talk to a friend or a professional about it instead of reading a self-help book. While they might say the same things, talking to someone will probably make you feel better and you'll be more likely to act on the information. Reading a self-help book, though, will most likely just get you stuck in your head. Don't do that to yourself. Ask for help.

If you have problems, then just start working on them. Trust me, you don't need to be reading self-help for that. Just start helping yourself. No one is going to come to fix your problems for you. But the good news is you can improve your life. So start doing exactly that. If you have a toothache, see a dentist. If you have back problems, see a doctor. If you need money for something, take a loan.

If you need a friend, start talking to people. And if you don't know what to do with your life, ask someone for advice. Ask for help. Any problem can be solved, but you have to be the one to work on it. And if the first dentist did a bad job, then find one to redo the work. If that doctor doesn't help, then see another. If that bank is giving you bad rates, go to the next one or look online. If the person you are trying to be friends with, is treating you badly, then spend your time with someone who doesn't. If the person you asked for help gave you no advice or bad advice, then ask someone else. Don't let little things like that stand in your way. It's up to you to fix your own life. No book can help you with that. But don't stress about it.

Just start doing it without emotional pressure. Sure, you might not go about it the best way, but it's better than doing nothing at all. And the more time you spend on it, the more you'll figure things out and the sooner you'll fix your problem. Remember, change is a gradual process, so just more of a reason to start now. And don't waste your time reading self-help. That's energy and effort you could be using to fix your problem. Just start working on your problems. Help yourself.

Real self-help is just as the word implies, you help yourself. You exercise. You start that business. You make that call. And so on. But then reading self-help is the exact opposite of self-help. That is time and energy you could have used to help yourself. Remember, there is no secret to be found in those self-help books. That means you don't need to be reading them. You just have to put in the work. You just have to help yourself. And I think most people turn to self-help because the changes they are looking for don't come soon enough. That's understandable. But when you exercise, it takes months before you see any real results. A business could take years before you start making good money. And real friendships and relationships in general don't happen overnight. Change takes time. You just have to realize and appreciate that fact of life. And you do that by putting in the work and having faith that things will get better. And it will if you keep at it. So stop wasting your time reading self-help and start doing some real self-help. Try to help yourself.

You Already Know this. You already know all this stuff. There is nothing new under the sun. Most of self-help is common sense or stuff you can, or already have, figured out on your own. And things that are somewhat unique (it is better to give than receive, count your blessings, it's not what you know but who you know, etc.) you've already heard of in some form or another. So why do you keep consuming books that take hours to read that just repeats the same stuff? That's time you could be spending on actually improving your life. If you enjoy reading, then read some novels or educational stuff but not things that will make you think life is harder than it really is, not stuff that will get you stuck in your head.

Again, we're all unique individuals. What one self-help author writes about is what worked for them or, worst of all, what they think you want to hear. And guess what? They figured it out on their own. Rarely does one self-help book contribute its main idea to another self-help book. So how did that author figure it out on their own? By trying new things, by doing different stuff, by experimenting and experience, not by reading self-help. They applied a little bit of common sense and common knowledge to their life and learned what worked for them. They used their own brain to figure things out. And you can do the same. You already know this stuff; you just need to start applying it. You just need to start doing it. Besides not reading self-help, I know I didn't cover too much about what you shouldn't be doing with your life, so you might be tempted to read about those items in a book even though deep down you already know them. But even if we did cover them that's too much information for you to remember.

A better strategy is to focus on doing the good things, the positive things, the three steps, taking action, and you should naturally not do the bad ones. *Don't teach this stuff.* You might be tempted to hold on to self-help so you can teach what you've learned to others. So you can give them knowledge and so they won't have to make mistakes and learn it the hard way like you have. But that motivation is a selfish one. The real reason you're doing it is to justify your pain in learning it and to say it wasn't all just a waste of time. But it was.

You shouldn't be pushing ideas on people. And teaching self-help is pushing your ideas on them. Remember to honor their individuality and personal intelligence. We all need help, but don't assume you know their life and what it needs better than they do. If you want to give, if you really want to help people, you have to ask them what they need first. Don't assume they need your self-help material or that you know what they need in life. Instead, ask them if they need help and, if they need help, ask them what they need. And don't forget to honor the individuality in yourself. You're still learning and growing. You're a human being. You still make mistakes. So don't act like a Guru.You will just get more depressed when you mess up. Don't waste your time teaching people what you've learned in life because you're still learning. That's time you could be using to know more about yourself and the world around you.

Besides, those you teach won't really know what you're talking about until they learn it from firsthand experience. You should worry about you. If people ask for help or advice, that's one thing, but you need to be concerned about your own life first (like I said, do the three steps in order). And, trust me, when you focus on growing as an individual and doing what you're meant to do, it's often the best way to serve others. Give the gift of being your true yourself to others. I'm not saying to not give help to others. It's all about giving in the right way. Which, honestly, can be hard to figure out. But part of it that I'm certain about is being true to yourself. And if being a teacher isn't who you really are, then don't do it. Fix your life first. Be a success then you can tell others how you made it. But you're not a Guru at life so don't pretend to be one. And don't tell people you're not a Guru and then try to teach them like you are one. It's a waste of your time and theirs. Focus on your own journey. Let the real world be your teacher and theirs.

Don't get me wrong, I have nothing against teaching. It is a wonderful profession that helps people. But what I'm saying is to not teach out of insecurity or the need to feel validated. Be true to yourself. Besides pushing your ideas onto people, the big problem with teaching is that you think you're taking action. You're not. Don't let it fool you. You'll never improve your life that way. Remember, action is the only thing that'll save you. Besides, there are plenty of people teaching this stuff already. We don't need another book even another one that tells you to stop reading self-help books. Worry about yourself. Let other people teach. Your job is to act. *Be True to Yourself.* Probably the fastest way to get rid of this self-help trash is to just be true to yourself. Don't follow some system or someone's ideas on life. It'll just drain you. Instead, do what feels right—not what feels pleasurable, necessarily, but what feels right to you.

Trust your gut. Even if the three steps don't feel right to you, then stop doing them and if you do what feels right, trust me, you'll naturally end up doing the three steps anyway. I would still suggest you start by doing the three steps for a period of time as these new actions will create new feelings in you. And those feelings will help to show you who you truly are. But if you really don't plan on doing the three steps, then at the very least focus on getting out of your house to try new things and talking to new people. Do that enough and you'll start moving towards the things and the people that make you feel good and away from things and people that don't. Life will start to feel right. You'll start to be your true self. Help yourself.

And if you're being true to yourself, you'll admit that you don't want to spend your time alone anymore. You'll admit you want to interact with other people. You'll admit you need more genuine conversation and connection in your life. You'll admit that you want to be with your group. But it's up to you to find them and putting on a mask given by a self- help book will just get in the way. In other words, just keep putting yourself out there and be yourself. Help yourself and be true to yourself. Help yourself by being true to yourself. Relax. Don't stress about life. You don't have to be putting on a facade and you don't have to act a certain way around people. Be true to your feelings and you'll figure it all out along the way. That's how life is meant to be played. And that's all you have to do. If putting yourself out there isn't working for you, it's because you aren't talking to people. And if you aren't talking to people, then you aren't being true to yourself.

We're social creatures. And if you are talking to people and are still stuck it's because you aren't opening up enough about your life and your problems or you aren't opening up to the right people. Ask for help. Really all you need to do is to get out of your own way. (And reading, thinking about, or even writing self-help is causing you to get in your own way. And you get out of your own way by just doing what needs to be done, by letting go of self-help, by finally taking action, by doing what your heart has been calling you to do.) You just need to stop overthinking things and just do whatever you've been thinking about. Be true to yourself. Get out of your own way; stop reading self-help. Get out of your own way; just do whatever you've been thinking about. There's a disconnect in your mind... between what you want and what you do. And that's why you keep running back to self-help... you're hoping to bridge that gap between fantasy and reality.

But that won't work. Only by acting on your thoughts will you start to connect your mind and fix your life. The secret isn't to think about what you want. The secret is to act on what you think about. (But if they're evil thoughts, you're not being true to yourself for in the hearts of all men and women is goodness, but some just have theirs buried under a lot of garbage.) Action will let you know the true nature of reality. Action will tell you who you really are. It won't be easy, acting on your thoughts, as fear is the chasm between what you want and what you do. But the more you do it the easier it becomes. Don't think twice about doing it. Don't let fear and indecisiveness hold your back in life. But keep in mind, spending time with people will make it more likely you'll bridge those two worlds. So don't be staying in your room alone. And talking to people, especially good people, about your thoughts/plans will make you more likely to act on them. Start being social. So stop putting things off by reading self-help. Nothing will go perfect in life, but you can only really learn and change from doing. Help yourself.

If you ever find yourself letting your imagination run riot living in fantasy worlds, or making big plans that you never act on, stop yourself and starting acting on those thoughts instead. No matter what kind of thoughts they are you can always act on in some shape or fashion. The three steps are just a more detailed plan for those having a hard time figuring things out. And that's probably because you're trying to do life all alone, which itself is usually a dysfunctional byproduct of reading self-help material. Doing things alone isn't natural/your true self. Remember, isolation is the dream killer. Be a real human being for once—do what feels right—and go be around others. Go interact with the real world. It may not be good idea during these corona times but rest assured it will pass.

It all comes down to being true to yourself. Even if you are socially awkward from being so isolated, put yourself out there. Like working out a muscle, you'll get better at it the more you do it. You won't notice the change right away, but it will happen if you keep at it.A lot of people say who you surround yourself with determines your success more than anything. But you won't find those people, good, helpful people who want to be around you, if you don't keep putting yourself out there and be yourself around people (don't be putting on a self-help mask). And since you shouldn't have to work on being yourself (being nervous and shy is natural in new situations but that will also naturally go away the more you put yourself out there), it really is all a matter of putting yourself out there.

As has been said in a similar fashion, success in life is pretty much all about showing up, it's about putting yourself out there. That's how most people are successful in life, they just put themselves out there, and they just show up to things. They don't waste their time in life reading self-help books. Many describe their successful life as something they fell into it, their job, their friends, etc. But it didn't happen by happenstance. Normal, productive people put themselves out there and they talk to other people about their lives. Remember, talk about your problems as you'll learn far more from other people than you will from any self-help book.

Communicate.

And if you put yourself out there and interact with the world, trust me, it'll feel right. But you can't put yourself out there if you're in your room on the computer. Now it doesn't mean everything you show up to will be a success, but if you put yourself out there enough you'll figure out who you are, what you really like to do, and who you like to spend your time with. You'll find success eventually, but only if you keep putting yourself out there. (Remember, isolation is the dream killer. Don't let yourself be alone). Putting yourself out there will help you from getting stuck in your head. Putting yourself out there will help you from being too serious about life. Putting yourself out there will help you find opportunities. Putting yourself out there will help to bridge fantasy to reality. Putting yourself out there will help to push things along. Putting yourself out there will help to build your intuition, your gut feeling about things.

And that'll help you to make better decisions in life. But to build that intuition, you need life experiences and true life experience comes from interacting with others, not just simply going to new places alone. Talk to people. So when you get invited to something, go. If someone is going somewhere, tag along. And go to that class, take that cruise, fly to that country, apply for that job—do whatever it is you've been thinking about. You'll never know what will come of it unless you go. Sure, not everything will be fruitful; but if you keep putting yourself out there you'll eventually find friends, fun, success, and fulfilment. Your fantasies will start to become a reality. But you won't find it in those self-help books, videos, podcasts, your daydreams, your secret plans, or whatever is causing you to stay in your room.

You have to get out of your room and meet people to find out who you really are. Keep putting yourself out there and you'll find who you truly are. How to Change.Face it. You are turning to self-help for some kind of change. And you're probably looking for a quick fix (though I doubt you can admit that to yourself), but life doesn't work out that way. It's a gradual process. But if you knew that, or at least accepted it, then you wouldn't be turning to self-help or trying to implement some crazy idea. Instead, you would just start doing the work and start using your current resources because you know you have a long road ahead of you, not try to find some hidden idea or strategy in a self-help book. Doing things all at once doesn't work. You have to do it gradually, very gradually.

And what you need to do gradually is the right thing, the three steps.

Communicate, take action, help others, etc. and basically, all the good stuff you've been taught growing up. And aiming to change means you probably won't (at least not in the way you want to). Aiming to do the right thing, however, means you probably will. So don't try to do a big change because you probably won't succeed and it'll leave you worse off.

Remember, planning, at least by yourself, is often planning to fail. Instead, focus on doing the right thing each day. And doing the right thing means being true to yourself. Believe it or not, it's true. And if you think it isn't, then you've been out of tune with your real feelings for way too long. And being your true self means communicating when you need help, being a good person, and connecting to others. I'm not against making a big change in your life. We've all heard of people, personally or on the news, who have done it. But they were successful and were able to make a big change because they were being true to themselves.

They didn't do it because they were trying to change themselves. They didn't do it because they were copying someone else. Be true to yourself, do the right thing, and change will naturally come.

Remember, you can't plan for things by yourself. So planning by yourself for a big change means you're just going to fail at it. You might gain some new understanding of yourself, but all you'll really gain is understanding what a mistake it was.

You have to take advantage of your opportunities when they present themselves. You can't really make them (all you can do is find them). So when opportunities present themselves, you have to take advantage of them. And you take advantage of them by doing the right thing, by doing the three steps. In short, you don't know what you don't know.

Until you do something, you don't know if it's a good idea or not, if an opportunity exists. So take action and find out. Don't waste your time planning for your big change. Help yourself, get help from others, and see if people want what you have to offer. Again, follow the three steps. In a way, you have to accept the world for what it is. Remember, you can't make opportunities, you find opportunities. If you could make opportunities you would be God. You're not God. When you run to self- help or try to use their strategies you're trying to make opportunities out of thin air. You're rejecting the world. But doing so won't change anything. You're just hurting yourself. Instead, accept the world for what it is and work with it. Play your part, use your relationships, use your gifts, use your feelings, be true to yourself, and enjoy and embrace the life you have. You can't control what happens to you but you can control how you respond.

Life is all about responding to it. Life is meant to be engaged, not studied. Life is meant to be learned from, not read about. Do what is best for yourself in the moment. Interact with life. Help yourself.

Self-help escapism will just get in the way of that. Follow the three steps instead. Start doing the right thing in your current situation, don't fight it. Your life depends on you doing the right thing. Like a plant in the sun, if you water it daily, it'll start to flourish. If not, it'll dry up and die. But even after you accept the world as it is, it's a slow process to change your life for the better. You might think you're an independent person, but, whether you like it or not, you depend entirely on your relationships. You have roots established where you live. If you want to grow as a person, you need new roots or to deepen your existing ones. But like any plant, it takes time to grow. Changing your life isn't going to come from the flip of a switch. So change isn't going to come from one big move or executing some master plan. Instead, start where you are. Begin today. If you want a better life you have to lay down new roots or improve the ones you have. And you do that by doing the right thing. And the three steps can help with that.

Unfortunately, that means giving up self-help will probably be a gradual process for you as well. But keep at it. Focus on taking action instead. Catch yourself when you're about to read some self-help and replace it with helping yourself and asking for help. Focus on doing the three steps. Just start doing the three steps. And be patient. Patience is a virtue. I know it's hard but good things really do come to those who wait. The overall point is if you plan on doing something crazy to improve or fix yourself: don't! Real change, or at the very least good change, can only really come gradually. There might be a build up to a major event, but the process to get there is still a gradual one. And you slowly get there by doing the right thing, by thinking the right thoughts, and by working with the right people.

Don't underestimate people when it comes to having a better life. They are the roots that let your plant (your life) grow and without them you will die. Stop spending all your time alone. But if you are going to do something crazy, if you're going to make some big change in your life, do it as a group. Take your roots with you. Don't go it alone. Ask for help. Still, it's a gradual process to get what you want. And you get there by being true to yourself, by doing the right thing, by doing the three steps. And if you focus on that, if you focus on your relationships, then one day change and happiness will suddenly be there. But, of course, change takes action; it's the only way to get there. So don't sit on your ideas (your thoughts).

Sitting on your ideas is the worst thing you can do. Always best to try out your idea and let the real world teach you what you need to know, not create a fantasy world around your ideas. You don't sit on your ideas; you act on your ideas. But action can be a funny thing. Action is the most important thing in life, but we always find ways or excuses to put it off. What you need is motivation to take action. Sure, you have to start with motivating yourself. You can't be wasting your time waiting for or searching for motivation. But real motivation always starts within, like striking a match within yourself. Remember, your burning desire must be found within as you are a unique individual.

But to have a roaring fire you need some outside fuel, you need to add some wood to that match.

To take a good amount, a healthy amount, of action, you need emotion, that's the fuel that motivates you to take action. Actions themselves do release emotions which will allow you to take more action, so better to help yourself/act than to think about things or to wait to be in the mood. But simply taking action gives diminishing returns when it comes to emotions. Best to get an unlimited amount of emotional fuel, like the near-infinite energy from the burning sun used by plants, to supply your actions. And that fuel for you is other people. It could be the beauty or love of a man or woman. It could be the peer pressure of, or the fun of being with, your friends. It could even be the hatred of, or wanting to impress, someone you have to see in person.

Whatever it is, the people in your life are your strongest motivator and creator of emotional fuel. And interacting with them on an electronic device is a poor substitute for the stimulation found from interacting with them in person. We're social creatures; start acting like it. Put the focus on others. Put yourself out there. Get involved in your community. I guarantee that'll give way to change. If you're not a student and you don't have a job, then get one. Just choose one that feels right to you with the right people. And if you're a student, join a few clubs on campus. Even if you've done that before, don't give up on finding one that clicks. Even a minimal paying, part- time one is a better than nothing.

And if you're having a hard time finding a job, tell the people closest to you that you're looking for one. You'll be surprised how much they can help. But they can't help if they don't know. Ask for help. Besides, earning money is a good, but not an absolute, measure of how much value you are providing to society. Thus, earning some money with a part-time job is often better than earning no money in your room. Plus, a job forces you to take action almost daily. So it helps to put you in an active state in life instead of a passive one like when you watch TV.

And when you get more experience (you work) and you choose to experiment in life (you try different jobs), you'll eventually find a job that not only pays more but fulfills you more, that makes you happy. And that helps to break you out of learned helplessness. And if you want to be self-employed, chances are if you can't do it on the side while working on your full-time job, you won't be able to do it as your main job, you don't have the discipline yet. So start with a paying job first, especially one that'll teach you about the job you want while self-employed, and do your own job on the side until you can slowly transition. If not, you might get stuck in a routine where you aren't earning any real money with it and relying on welfare or your parents to pay your bills, where you aren't providing any real value to society. Don't do that to yourself. People won't respect you. Help yourself.

But it all starts with that first job, even a part-time one. It all starts with you getting out of your room. So start with a low paying job, at least you know you are adding value to society, and work your way up from there. And at the very least it will get you out of your room and into the real world. Trust me, you'll feel better about yourself. You'll get to know people in your community instead of just staying on your computer. And the more involved you get with your community the sooner you'll move up in life. I know you want to be self-employed; you want to be your own boss. But the only successful people I've seen do that transition from a full time job first.

To be successful in a self-employed job, you have to know not only what people's desires/demands are, but you also have to find them and convince them you can provide what they are looking for. And this knowledge isn't easy to come by. And often you still can't do that entirely alone. In other words, you need a team. But no one will partner with or work under you until you first have a proven track record. With rare exception, most learn it from a full-time job in that area. Then they take that knowledge (and possibly clients) to their own job or, at the very least, take their skill set they learned from that job to applicable work in self-employment, though this is less common as it is harder to pull off since you don't have that deep knowledge of that particular industry like where to find and keep clients.

There are exceptions, but it is so rare it would be silly to think you fall into this group. Remember how I said to let the world teach you what to give? Well, it's already telling you what it wants by all the jobs that need to be filled. Now you just need to figure out which job you can give the best at. And you do that by experience and experimenting. You experiment by working different jobs. And once you find one that best suits your personality and gain enough experience in it, then you can go work for yourself. Even if you plan on doing sales on your own where you actively reaching out to people to find that demand, it's still best to work under someone first and then go work on your own.

And if you plan on doing some internet work to avoid the normal workforce, it's still best to work under someone who is really good at it first and then work on your own. You want that deep knowledge, skill set, confidence, and even relationships before you venture off. Don't get me wrong, there are plenty of people who did it entirely on their own. But they are a rather tiny, microscopic group compared to all the failures out there who had to give up. And to think that you belong to that rare group is a little foolish. Even if you do belong to that rare group who can do it, you are still better off working under someone first as you'll move further fast and be more likely to be successful and then go work for yourself. And your job doesn't have to have anything to do with your dream. It can be a means to an end. But pursue your dream (not your fantasy worlds) on your off time. You can, if it is advantageous to you, eventually make your job or self-employment about your dream. But for now just get a job, then you can do your money making dream. Besides, remember that focusing on others will help you with your dreams more than anything else. Get a job.

Bottom line is you need to work for someone first before you can earn the right to work for yourself (at least it is healthier to think of it that way). Humble yourself and work for someone else. And if you don't like the industry, work environment, the people in it, or have an abusive boss, quit (help yourself) and then find another job (again, help yourself... stop avoiding things). But don't try to do some type of "self-employment" to run away from work and the real world. Remember, you earn self-employment from the knowledge, skills, confidence, and relationships you get from working under someone else. Don't try to skip this step or you'll not only probably fail but make yourself miserable in the process. Help yourself. Get a job. Trust me, you'll feel better about yourself when you do.

Besides, like I said, having a job (even a part-time job) allows you to get to know people in your community. In summary, your job in life is to, remember, and serve others. But you first have to find that demand. The beautiful thing about applying for a job is that you know there is a demand for that service or else there wouldn't be a job to apply for. But with self-employment it's hard to find that demand, it's hard to know that you're providing value to society. And society expects you to be a producer before you become a consumer, if not, trust me, people won't like you. People are smarter than you think. While the money you earn isn't the absolute measure of how much value you are providing to society, it is a pretty good measure and the vast majority of people in society will judge you by it. Imagine being in a job you hate with long hours and you see someone taking advantage of the government or their parents to make their way in life. If you put yourself in their shoes you know it would be hard for your emotions to not get the best of you. So get a job, even a temporary, less-than-ideal, part-time job and then work your way up to a full-time job you'd prefer to have with better pay, and master it until, and if you want to, work for yourself.

And don't be afraid to quit a bad job as well. Just make sure to get a new one right away. But humble yourself first by working for someone. And while you're doing it you'll know you're adding value to society, you'll be doing your part in serving others. And if you're having a hard time getting one, keep applying. You'll find one eventually. Remember, change is a gradual process. But you need people's help. And getting a job, or a new one, is a good way to get people into your life, to get the right people into your life, and to give to others. It's a good way to stop spending all your time alone in your room and to start getting to know people in your community. That is the path to change. But most important of all, and I saved the best for last, a job will help you find friends. Get a job. Help yourself.

Relax. Finally, I want you to relax. I know I said a lot in this book, but all you have to do is the three steps. In other words, take action and spend time with your friends. Don't stress out about changing your life or doing the three steps. Just don't let yourself forget about the three steps either. And a reminder can take care of that for you. The world is still going to be there no matter what you do. No need to rush things. Everything has its time and place. And trying to hurry things along will just hurt your progress. And if you're in real trouble, go get some help! Other than that, I don't see anything in life worth worrying about. So don't take it so seriously. Relax and have some fun with your life. Go have an adventure.

I can't say it enough, with the three steps you just need to ease into it when doing them. everything is going to be okay. And if you can have fun when doing the three steps, even better. All you have to do in life is the right thing. And, no, it isn't that hard. Communicate, speak up when something is bothering you, ask for help, think good thoughts, surround yourself with good people, be a good person, remove yourself from toxic situations, don't let your life become boring, don't take yourself so seriously, give to others, help others, etc. But you already know all this stuff. Life isn't that hard as long as you're doing the right thing.

There is no secret formula to not worry about. You just need to start applying some common sense to your life. As long as you do the right thing every day, that's all that matters as you'll slowly move closer to the life you desire. But stressing out about it won't help things along. If anything, it'll also hurt your progress. Remember, life is to be enjoyed. Relax. Ease into the three steps, start doing the right thing. Next time you go to a library don't distract yourself with self-help material and start being true to yourself. There is nothing there you don't already know, and there is nothing there that is going to help you. You need to start relying on yourself to take the right action. You just need to help yourself and get the help of a friend. A book will just get in the way of that. So don't give in.

The same goes for anything you find online. Instead of giving in and clicking that link, tell yourself, "This material will just get in my way. I just need to do what needs to be done." And do it. Perhaps you think this is too extreme, but would you harass an alcoholic for having a not-even-one drink policy? Of course not. What about a person who wants to be healthy using that same policy? I don't know about you, but I wouldn't hold it against them. Chances are if you decided to read this book, you need that same policy. So I dare you to walk pass that self-help aisle of the bookstore and when you start walking around you'll realize you have more time and energy to be yourself, to do the things you want to do, to be who you were meant to be.

Don't Be Alone. I hate to tell you this since you are almost done reading the book, but the three steps probably won't work for you. If you're the type to read this book in the first place, then you will either not try the three steps and reading another book or you'll make yourself miserable doing the three steps. Like all the other self-help garbage you tried, you'll follow the system for a few days or maybe even a few weeks, but then you'll either won't try it out or you'll make yourself miserable doing it. You'll get burned out and then try some other self-help garbage found in another book. But that's okay... Relax. I don't want you to follow the three steps; I want you to do the three steps. Remember how I said most people naturally do the three steps without realizing it by being with others? Remember how I said most of your problems came from trying to do life by yourself? The more time you spend with others the more likely you'll do the three steps and thus be successful in life.

And if your problems didn't come from not being social enough, then you either need to start forcing yourself to do the three steps or seek professional help. Probably both. When you're with people, they'll put peer pressure on you to take action in life, to help yourself. When you're with people, you'll be more likely to ask for help when you need it. When you're with people, you'll be more likely to put the focus on them and give to them. But when you spend your time alone, you'll be more likely to spin your wheels, you'll be more likely to get lost in your thoughts, and you'll be more likely to live in your own little world instead of the real world. Don't do that to yourself. Be social. Put yourself out there.

But when you're social, you might have to make a conscious effort to apply the three steps. Yes, you should naturally be more likely to do the three steps by being social. But if you're been antisocial for a while then you probably need a little push from yourself to start taking advantage of social situations, to start doing the three steps. And a written reminder that you see often can help you with that. And when you're with people, remember to put the focus on others. Put the focus on their wants and desires. But when you're with people, also be willing to speak up about what is bothering you. Make sure everyone's problems and desires are out on the table. I guarantee a lack of communication is at the root of all your problems.

And you can't give your best to others, you can't serve your community the best, if you're stuck with or nagging problems of your own. Plus, this way you don't get stuck in your head. Don't just sit in the corner. Speak up. And if you keep at it, you'll get there, it'll become second nature. So if the thing that's most likely to get you to do the three steps is being social and being social has a ton of other benefits for your physical and mental health, your career success, your happiness, and probably a lot of other things not mentioned here. Taken to its logical conclusion you should maximize the amount of time you spend with people each day and minimize the amount of time you spend alone each day.

Put yourself out there. When you do your work, do it with other people. When you eat, do it with people. When you do your fun activities, do it with people. Sure, we all need our alone time, but that should be the occasional exception to the rule, not the rule itself. So how do you start? Start small; start where you are. Leave your door open. Real change, at least good, healthy change, has to happen organically and slowly. And the best way to do that is to start with where you live. Leave your door open. Stop reading self-help articles and just leave your door open. Let the real world in. I think you'll be amazed at the results. You can hide from the real world, but it'll get you sooner or later and you won't like it when it does. Or you can start letting the real world in now. Help yourself.

Will you get hurt from time to time? Sure, but you'll grow from it and become stronger. But if you wait for the real world to come and get you, you might never recover. I know I already used my "if there is one thing you take away from this book let it be this..." statement already (pretty much once for each of the three steps) but change has to start small as it allows you to be consistent and consistency will get you results. And I think leaving your door open is a good, easy place for you to start. If you live in a dormitory, leave your door open when you're in your room let the room be open if possible as long as you are there. What do you need your door closed for? Open your door and let the light in. It'll only do you some good. Besides, the darkness and secrets will only hurt you in the end. Livein a home all alone? Sit outside and say Hi to people. Live in a home all alone but out in the middle of nowhere? Invite your closest neighbors to come over or you can move closer to civilization. It's important to be with people.

There's a reason why suicide rates are higher in remote areas, even with less harassment and beautiful scenery. And there's a reason why suicide rates are lower in crowded areas, even with more crime and ugly scenery. We're a social species; don't isolate yourself. What would you choose: momentary pleasure and more long-term misery or temporary discomfort and more long-term happiness? Obviously the latter. But when you choose to stay on your electronics devices or in your fantasies worlds instead of being with people, you're choosing the former. But when you're being social or working on yourself, you're choosing the latter.

Instead of watching TV, go have a good conversation with someone. You'll feel a lot better afterwards. Don't be a slave to pleasure. You're better than that. Start working on having a better life. Leave your door open. The sooner you start the sooner you'll start seeing results. Even better, get the TV and computer out of your room. Put it somewhere that you have to be around people. It'll help keep you from wasting your time on it. And, remember, if you get a job (even a part-time one) it'll get you around people, it'll make you be more social. I want to take an aside to talk about various forms of entertainment and how they are bad for you. You should really view the time you spend watching TV for your brain/mental health the same as eating junk food for your body/physical health. I would say 30 minutes of watching TV is the same as eating a slice of burger. So if you're watching 2-3 hours of TV a day... you can see why you're mental health and your life is so messed up.

Television trains you to be in a passive state. And that's why you probably don't take action in life as much as you should, that's why you don't help yourself. And be careful with all those online videos nowadays as the computer is becoming just like the television. Even if you only use the internet to read articles, all those ads, including the ones on TV, can't be good for you. Companies don't spend millions on advertisements for no reason. Besides, even when it comes to reading, it looks like we're not meant for the glow of the computer screen. However, reading (even printed books) can also be bad for you. That's one of the main points of this book. The problem with reading is that it also puts you in a passive state. The proof is in all the self-help books people read without even using the material or not making proper use of the material they read. Worse and unlike TV, it can brainwash you into thinking/feeling that you're being productive with your time. While reading workout books won't fool anyone into thinking they're growing muscles while reading, intellectual and self-help books can have quite the treading water effect on your life.

Even if you do make reading into more of an active exercise (you take notes while you read, you write things down on your to-do list, or you act on the material right away), there is no promise that it'll do you any good. In fact, there is a very good chance it'll do you no good at all and just be a waste of time. Why? Because we are all unique individuals. What works for the author might not work for you (at least not in the long run). Best to learn on your own through experience and experimenting (help yourself) and to learn from those close to you in a similar situation or who have already gone through what you're going through (ask for help). Don't get me wrong, reading is clearly better for the brain than television; however, that doesn't mean it is the best use of your time compared to other things (like asking for help or just trying things out).

Opportunity cost applies to everything, even reading. A job, even a part-time one, or working with or under someone will often teach you more than a book, or even a bunch of books, ever will. While the television, online videos, and reading can be great tools to gather knowledge when you need it, don't let your tools become your masters. Don't let these fantasy worlds (online material, television, books, or even your daydreams) give you solutions, wants, and desires that don't really exist inside you or don't really work out in the real world. Forget the illusion. Let the real world teach you what it is that you really want, what you should be doing with your life, and try things out to see if they are the answers you are looking for.

That's the only way to really learn or to live. Perhaps you graduated from watching TV all day to reading books all day. That's better. You should be proud of yourself. But now it's time to graduate to taking action all day, to interacting with the real world, to being around people. So stick to interacting with the real world (you can still read books, especially the paper ones... just not the self-help ones, as long as you're also interacting with the real world). Don't make yourself sick with TV and online videos. Don't live entirely in your fantasy worlds. So don't stay in your room all day long, even if you are reading a book. So open your door and let the real world in.

Open your door and let your community in. Leaving your door open will also help you to bring the fantasy in your mind into the reality of your world as your fantasy has nowhere to hide anymore. And that's a very good thing. After all, don't you want to make your fantasies into reality? You can choose to stay in your room and rot with your secret plans. Or you can let the light in (let other people into your life) and slowly start to flourish. When people visit your house, come out and spend time with them. Even if you don't say anything, it'll do you some good. (But do try to add to the conversation). And when people invite you to things which will happen more often if you have your door open, say yes. Sure, there's a chance you won't enjoy it. But nothing is perfect in life; however, the more you put yourself out there the more likely you'll find what you're looking for.

The three steps are still important. But they're more of a guide for the socially awkward. So if you aren't getting the results you want in life from being social, now you know why and what to apply. So start with the first step. Help yourself. Leave your door open and start talking to people. Now you might get the urge to close your door. Don't. Change won't come overnight. Change doesn't happen right away. But keep at it. Keep your door open and you will see results. Remember, patience. Good things will come in time. Leave your door open. Conclusion. Before I give the conclusion, let me give you a slightly different way to view things in this book.

I did promise I wouldn't talk about religion again, but here is my own personal (spiritual) belief. All is one. That means, helping another is no different than helping yourself. Helping yourself is no different than helping another. This way of living can be hard to wrap your head around. But it can be done if you practice it by helping yourself and helping others, by loving yourself and loving others. But what about evil? By this logic, should you cut evil some slack? You could argue if you don't cut evil down it will surely cut down another. But all is one. Cutting down evil is no different than cutting down yourself. The difference between good and evil is what will last and what will not. The difference between good and evil is those who are suffering and those who are not. Do not add to another person's suffering. Let nature take its course and you show yourself kindness.

The Universe and love will take care of things. So all that really matters in life is love. That's all there really is, to love and be loved, to receive unconditionally and give unconditionally. But you have to make that decision to start loving unconditionally, you have to help yourself. So I said all you really need in life is to help yourself, ask for help, and give help to others. Another way to view it is to love yourself and do the actions that will benefit you and love others (go interact with and help them because that's the thing that really makes them happy). Friends are really the only thing you've been missing in your life. You don't need self-help when you have friends. And friendship is all about love: unconditional acceptance, unconditional giving and receiving, and caring for each other. Love yourself and love others. Take care of yourself, but put your attention on your friend's happiness, not yours, because that's how the world was designed to work.

If there is one thing I want you to take away from this book it's this (this one being the real one)... Don't focus on self-help; focus on helping others. Focus on others... I would even add that to your piece of paper with the three steps. Since we're at the end of the book, let's go over your reminder. It doesn't have to be a piece of paper; it just has to be something you'll see every day. At the very top it should have your big dream in life, then the three steps, and, finally, a reminder at the bottom to focus on/spend time with others. Because when you love people, that's what you do. You only ask for help because it helps others.

People want to see you make your dreams come true. It makes them happy to help you, they love doing it. But like I said, putting the focus on others, loving others, is a skill that must be developed. But you only develop that skill, like any skill out there, by doing it (or at least trying to do it) again and again, by helping yourself. You could say life is all about doing what needs to be done and making friends. And what needs to be done is for you to make (find) some friends. Remember, taking action and being with the right people is all that really matters in life. Loving others and being around the ones you love, that's all that matters in life. Anything else is just a distraction. And distractions will end up hurting you. And if there is really one good thing to take away from self-help material (besides taking action) it's the importance of others.

But doesn't that contradict the entire premise of self-help as the actions you should be taking shouldn't be about yourself but, rather, about others? Like I've said before, the real secret you'll find in self-help is there is no secret, so don't bother reading self-help. Instead, live your life and be a good person as everyone has been telling you to do this whole time. But how you be a good person, how you help others, how you find friends, how you show the world your love, how you live your life is really up to you to figure out on your own as you're a unique individual. And you figure it out by taking action. So don't fool yourself into thinking there is some self-help book or system that has the secret answer. Reading self-help will just get you lost in your thoughts. It will get you stuck in your head. And doing some weird self-help system will keep you from being yourself.

Again, the three steps aren't so much a system as

they are a friendly reminder to be proactive and social in life. But, hopefully, you'll get to the point where you don't even need the three steps anymore as a reminder to put the focus on others. Throw away the garbage that is self-help. Stop reading self-help. Just focus on doing what needs to be done.Please, I'm begging you. Stop reading self-help. And don't do it for yourself. Do it for those around you who need you to start being who you were meant to be. Start by helping yourself (getting out of your room), then ask people for help (being around people isn't enough, you need to communicate, let go of your ego and ask), and, finally, start giving back (because that's what you do for the people you love). But you have to do all three or else you'll get stuck in life, stuck in your head, or stuck with an empty feeling inside. And don't wait for when you have inspiration or when you feel good and don't read self-help hoping to find it. Don't wait for that perfect moment. Just focus on taking action.

Focus on loving others. The more you put yourself out there the sooner you're going to learn who you're supposed to be.

Don't get me wrong.

Things aren't going to be easy now that you have read this book, now that you know the steps, now that you know the truth. Working with the truth is the only way to really understand it. So don't be running back to this book or other self-help books when things go wrong, you make a mistake, or you get your feelings hurt. That's life. That's part of the learning process. The trick, and the only thing that really works in life, is to keep trying as you'll get better. But if you keep retreating, you'll just lose what momentum you've gained and you'll never really improve your life. Sure, you'll have bad experiences, feel bad emotions, come across bad people, or just feel sad or frustrated at times. But don't run back to self-help. You need to put yourself out there and figure things out for yourself. And you'll discover that all you really need to do is to find the courage to take the right action in life. Help yourself. Ask for help. Give help to others.

To stop doing the action is causing those bad things to happen. Action, not reading, is the answer. Help yourself. Make sure to stay on track. Put the focus on/act in regards to other people. They can often be the motivation you need to stop doing your bad habits in life and to start doing the rights ones. You can view it as working on creating long-term relationships, learning how to trust people again, facing your fears, being with those you love, loving the world, communicating with others, being social, putting yourself out there, showing up, being around good people, not letting yourself be isolated, or whatever. The important thing is that you keep the focus on others. Keep a reminder close to you (the three steps or whatever you come up with). And make sure you look at it every single day. Don't forget about it being in your wallet or your purse. Make an extra copy and keep it where you know you'll see it often. Use it to start shaping the new actions you're going to be taking in your new life. And don't stress about the three steps. All you have to do is focus on doing them when you can, focus on others. Don't worry about doing them perfectly. And don't worry about the results. They'll take care of themselves if you put in the work, if you do the three steps.

All you have to focus on is making them a part of your life. And don't reread this book. Please don't let it also get you sucked up into your own little self-help world. It's too much stuff to remember anyway, so it won't do you any good to reread it. But the three steps are easy to remember and they'll give you exactly what you want from life. Help yourself, ask for help, and give help to others. Just focus on using the three steps. Taking action is the only thing that'll save you. Besides, you'll internalize and learn on your own everything said in this book through firsthand experience by using the three steps, so don't worry about remembering what was said in it.

Just focus on taking action. Just focus on doing, or even trying to do, the three steps. Focus on connecting with others. Focus on being true to yourself. You'll get it sooner or later if you keep at it. And the best part is you'll find your own way in life without a self-help book holding your hand. There's nothing else to learn. There's nothing else to know. 109 You just need to get out of your own way. You need to stop reading self-help and start doing. It's time to go beyond self-help. It's time to start being honest with yourself. It's time to start engaging with the real world. It's time to let go of fear and start walking around naked as the person you're supposed to be. And love is who you've always been. It's time to connect.

Stop telling yourself you're broken inside and that you need to be fixed or that you need to improve yourself before you're worthy of love. You don't need self-help; you just need to start helping yourself. You just need to start engaging with the real world and stop escaping to the world of self-help. That's how you learn who you really are. It doesn't matter how many books or articles you read. You can't experience life unless you experience it. You can't change your life unless you change it. You can't live your life unless you live it. Put down the self-help. Books are no substitute for people or living the adventure called life.

But you can start small. Leave your door open when you're in your room and start talking to the people who come by. It'll add up! It's time to take responsibility for your life. It's time to forget the self-improvement and go after what you really want. It's time to start living the life you've always wanted instead of just reading about it. And what you want is connection. What you want are people who will accept you as you are, faults included. That's what unconditional love is. But you first have to make that choice to live in the real world. And it all starts with you putting down those self-help books.

The world is an an incredible place. All you have to do is begin. Love and be loved. Love yourself and love others. Loving yourself means letting go of what isn't good for you. Loving people means putting them first. Follow this path and I guarantee your life will change for the better. Let that be your final self-help advice. And let this be your last self-help book. Now tell yourself, "I'm done with self-help. Now I'm going to start living my life. And when I do need help I'm just going to ask for it instead. But now I'm going to start living my life for others." Help yourself. Ask for help. Give help to others.

Now get up and get going

CPSIA information can be obtained
at www.ICGtesting.com
Printed in the USA
BVHW071135240521
607998BV00004B/478